CLASSIC BUS
YEARBOOK – 5

ALCESTER LANES END
VIA BRADFORD STREET 50B

HOV 955

EDITED BY GAVIN BOOTH

Ian Allan
PUBLISHING

CONTENTS

First published 1999

ISBN 0 7110 2668 8

Design by Hieroglyph

Published by Ian Allan Publishing

an imprint of Ian Allan Publishing Ltd, Terminal House, Shepperton, Surrey TW17 8AS
Printed by Ian Allan Printing Ltd, Riverdene Business Park, Hersham, Surrey KT12 4RG

Code: 9904/B

INTRODUCTION

UNASHAMED NOSTALGIA is what the fifth *Classic Bus Yearbook* is all about, and we recognise that the interests of our readers cover not only all parts of the UK, but many different time-periods. Inevitably, fewer readers will have first-hand experience of the buses of the 1920s and an increasing number will feel nostalgic about the 1970s and 1980s. We try to reflect this changing pattern in the Yearbook and in the bi-monthly *Classic Bus* magazine which inspired this book. When we started CB in 1992 we majored heavily on the 1950s and 1960s, but in response to readers' requests, we have rolled on into more recent times. While buses of the 1970s are still to be found in reasonable numbers, today very few look the way they did when they were new, as some of the photos in the book remind us.

The pleasures of early bus-spotting expeditions by bike are recalled by Mike Lloyd, who ventured into the Home Counties in the 1960s, and at the other end of the country Peter Myers found himself teaching in Caithness in 1979-81, and recalls the Highland fleet that worked in this remote area. R. J. Williamson found himself on holiday in Clacton in 1959, when holiday demand for buses and coaches was still very high, and describes the efforts made by Eastern National to move the crowds.

Philip Wallis took his camera to a very different Heathrow in 1971 and captured on film the vehicle variety that served the airport even then. Another regular CB contributor, Michael Dryhurst, considers the year 1958 in London – not a happy year, and one that was to prove a turning point in London Transport's fortunes.

Three features look at municipal transport. Geoff Burrows considers the influence tramway managers had on bus design, and Thomas Knowles recalls working at Derby Corporation during the final stages of the change-over from trolleybuses to motorbuses. David Harvey tells the story of Birmingham's fleet of Daimler CVD6s, a type that never quite lived up to its promise.

The connections between aircraft manufacturing and bus bodybuilding are considered by Gerald Truran, who looks particularly at the brief but successful foray into bus bodies by Saunders and Saunders-Roe.

And lovers of the offbeat will enjoy a characteristic Robert Jowitt article, taking a sidelong glance at buses and their uses in later life.

There are photo-features – Alan Townsin dips into John Smith's album to reveal some unusual photos, and the buses and liveries of Northern General and its associate companies are covered in black-and-white and colour Photobus photos.

Many enthusiasts collect old picture postcards featuring buses and trams, and Peter and Judy Deegan have selected cards from their extensive collection showing charabancs and other early coaches and buses on the Isle of Man; still popular with transport enthusiasts, the island was a hugely successful tourist attraction in the days before cheap foreign travel.

Several regular features from *Classic Bus* magazine appear in the Yearbook, including instant information in Checkpoint style, John Aldridge's I Was There recollections, Chassis Code Cracking and Open Platform.

These features, plus articles and photo-features from the best writers and photographers around, appear in the bi-monthly magazine *Classic Bus*. If you have enjoyed this book, you will enjoy the magazine.

Gavin Booth

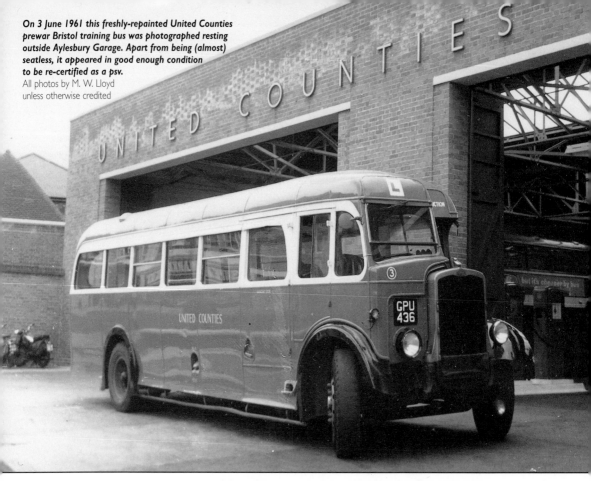

On 3 June 1961 this freshly-repainted United Counties prewar Bristol training bus was photographed resting outside Aylesbury Garage. Apart from being (almost) seatless, it appeared in good enough condition to be re-certified as a psv.
All photos by M. W. Lloyd unless otherwise credited

BUS-SPOTTING BY BIKE

M. W. LLOYD explored the Home Counties in the 1960s, complete with bike, friend, Tizer and Kodak Cresta camera

LIKE SO MANY teenage bus-spotters in the 1960s, I was not flush with cash and relied on the combination of leg-power and my trusty Raleigh bicycle to take me to the far-away exotic buses of towns in my area. Many of my cycle trips were solo, but on occasions I had a companion in the shape of a fellow enthusiast from the same school as me. With my notebook, sandwiches, bottle of Tizer and a fifty-bob (£2.50) Kodak Cresta camera I explored the Home Counties from my base at Hemel Hempstead. This article takes a composite view of my journeys northwards to my favourite destination of Aylesbury.

The first few miles of any such trip would be of little interest. Passing through the village of Potten End I would follow the B&B Services route to Berkhamsted, almost always seeing somewhere their OB service bus plodding up and down with few passengers even then. The turn-off to the Bonar Law College at Ashridge might perhaps give a glimpse of its Bedford SBG/Duple Midland service bus VNK 763 in its attractive blue and cream livery disappearing down the tree-lined minor road leading to its base. This was an unusual vehicle in that it was a non-psv bus to full psv standards purchased new by the college in 1956; it later passed to Ronsway, Hemel Hempstead where I got to know it much better. On down the hill to

Top: *London Transport No T790 shows off the rear of its Mann Egerton body outside Berkhamsted station on 22 July 1961. The grassy mound in the background is part of the remains of Berkhamsted Castle, but the wooden hut beside the T is as much a memory as the bus itself.*

Above: *United Counties No 317, perhaps the archetypal rural bus, awaits departure from outside Tring LT Garage on 17 March 1962.*

Berkhamsted station where, if it happened to be a Saturday, there would be a real treat hiding by the old timber building which seemed to serve as a scout-hut. London Transport AEC Regal III No T790 was one of the very last of a class going back to the dawn of LT, and on one occasion I persuaded the family to travel on it to Dunstable just to sample the vehicle, the very first time I can recall riding on a bus for its own sake rather than to get somewhere. No T790 was a nice change from the masses of RTs and RFs, and it put in appearances until its sale in late 1963. I realised that it probably had very little in common with earlier members of the T class, but it gave a nice sense of historical perspective.

Berkhamsted itself offered little of bus interest except at lunch time or four o'clock in the afternoon when the Midland Red coach J came through, working its daily trip between Birmingham and London. Various examples of BMMO's home-made vehicles appeared over the years, and it was a bit of excitement when a C5 Motorway coach turned up, as they did sometimes.

Between Berkhamsted and Tring the open countryside was pleasant, and one might spy parked up an obscure lane an elderly halfcab coach carrying the workers on the electrification of the West Coast main line. One would certainly spy a stream of London Transport buses and Green Line coaches, but we had almost always spotted these already, and unless there

Above: *Midland Red No 5175, a Leyland Leopard with Willowbrook body, drops a passenger in Buckingham Street, Aylesbury on 26 October 1963. The basketwork Post Office barrow is a reminder of a form of local delivery now superseded.*

Left: *A chance encounter – Airtech of Haddenham Airport operated a number of former psvs as staff transport. On 9 September 1963 this Duple-bodied Maudslay, resplendent in blue livery, was parked on the road to Leighton Buzzard. The verdant land on the coach's nearside was the trackbed of the LNWR branch to Aylesbury, even then long disused.*

was a freshly-overhauled example, we would tend to ignore them. This incidentally raises the question of quite how you spot buses while bicycling, and the answer is simple. You coast, with one leg up, and rest your notebook on that leg while you scribble hastily! Sounds dangerous, but in those days of relatively little traffic we did it frequently with never a mishap.

'Foreign' operator

On reaching Tring we would take a breather and inspect the London Transport garage (now closed). You couldn't see much in this little place – perhaps a GS from Amersham waiting to return to Chesham via Wigginton, or a couple of red RTs used as Aldenham staff buses, but at Tring you did meet the first 'foreign' operator, for the town was served by United Counties. Its main line service was the 16 (later 61) Aylesbury to Luton, which generally featured LD and later FLF Lodekkas. I never took to the former, although the latter seemed quite nice; but the big attraction was the local services to surrounding villages, which used Bristol L single-deckers. These must be one of the classic good-looking traditional buses of all time, and it was nice to see them at work, complete with conductor and rear entrance with sliding door. Carrying only 35 passengers, they can hardly have been economical but

they were a very attractive alternative to the monotonous RFs!

Tring boasted an independent whose depot I never found, but whose fleet always included oddities. Jack Caterer's Icknield Coaches was named after the ancient Way which passed through Tring. The livery was 'previous owner's' and the fleet included one of those little Trojan 13-seaters that were popular in the early 1960s, a 16-seat Austin CVC with Kenex body, and KUY 536, an impressive rear-engined Foden with Metalcraft coachwork. Icknield Coaches no longer runs, but an Icknield Garage is still owned by the Caterer family.

Having refreshed ourselves we are ready to continue. There is a long pull out of Tring heading northwards, but once over the summit we enjoy a longer downhill stretch, cooling us off nicely as we run in to the long, straggling village of Aston Clinton. Nothing much of note here except a couple of coaching inns, The Bell and The Rising Sun whose origins go back well before internal combustion, and the factory in which are made Oriole Records and those curious 'Embassy' cover versions sold in Woolworths rather more cheaply than the real thing. The stretch of the A41 road between Tring and Aylesbury not only offers us more London Transport

City of Oxford AEC Regent/Northern Coachbuilders No 131 at Kingsbury Square, Aylesbury on 23 May 1961 not only displays the author's initials but also its elegantly-phrased blind. Note the splendid bus shelter.

and United Counties vehicles to spot but is also covered, according to the timetable, by a rail replacement service from Oxford to Cambridge described as 'Premier Travel and Percival's Coach 39' which only runs once a day in each direction and which, hard though it is to believe, I never managed to see, so we leave this to the imagination and hasten on to our destination along level roads through pleasant farming land until at last we reach the market town, and capital of Buckinghamshire, Aylesbury.

Feast of buses

Oh, Aylesbury, Kingsbury Square, what a feast of buses awaits there! Today the town resembles all others, with covered bus station, concrete shops, one-way systems – it might be anywhere; but at that time there was still a lot of character left before the developers did their worst (similar things could no doubt be written about Guildford, Winchester, Maidstone, etc . .). Kingsbury Square wasn't actually square in the literal sense, but it was a hub of the bus scene. In the middle was a large

City of Oxford single-deckers were renowned for the decorative vee-front mouldings. Willowbrook-bodied AEC Regal IV No 738 at Kingsbury Square on 14 June 1961 displays this attractive feature.

paved area with beautiful brick-built shelters, complete with ornamental ironwork on their roofs, substantial benches, windows with glass in (pre-vandalism days, these!) and a general air of quality. Timetables were displayed, stop signs were clearly marked, and everywhere were buses, interesting ones at that. One point did strike me then, as it still does. At Aylesbury, London Transport was very much the minority operator, with only two bus routes running into the Square (the Green Line coaches, for some reason, terminated outside the United Counties garage in Buckingham Street) so why were all the timetable cases, stop signs, etc., so obviously in the LT house style? Did some Aylesbury councillor admire the work of Frank Pick, or did London Transport simply shoulder their way to the front and impose their ideas anyway?

It didn't seem to matter, really. What did matter was the variety of buses on show. RTs in green livery were forgotten as soon as local independent Red Rover appeared. Its management certainly admired LT, for it bought a fleet of RTs, not to mention a solitary example each of RTL and RTW classes for its network of stage services centred on the town. Red Rover livery was a lovely dark red, almost maroon, with yellow relief and black wings – black roofs too, sometimes, and they had fleetnumbers. It also had an associate

company called Keith Coaches Ltd which had a similar livery. Crews in uniforms, Setright speed ticket machines – it all added up to a proper 'big-operator' image and when in April 1962 it purchased a brand-new AEC/Park Royal Bridgemaster (27 WKX) there was no doubt that this was a firm to be taken seriously. The full title, Red Rover Omnibus Ltd, intrigued me – no 'Company', still less 'Traction' or 'Road Car' – and I discovered that this was the last remnant of a former London 'pirate.'

We had met United Counties at Tring, but in Aylesbury there was no escaping them, with examples of the K and L families and the LS saloons seemingly going everywhere. Perhaps the least likely service in those days was the 141 which went, incredibly, all the way to far-off St Ives, and took nearly four hours to get there. Did anyone ever travel all the way, I wonder, and if so how on earth did they manage without refreshment stops? Most routes, however, were far less adventurous, and some never left the confines of the town. Tilling group buses made a change from my

United Counties No 734 originated with Eastern National. It is about to make the trip to Halton Hospital on 14 June 1961.

'native' green London Transport ones, but pride of my United Counties spottings was training bus No 3, a prewar Bristol L with the old-type sit-up-and-beg radiator which I photographed outside Aylesbury garage, freshly repainted, in August 1961. What a pity it did not survive into preservation.

Tilling was also represented at Aylesbury by Thames Valley whose red buses were in reality no different from the green ones of United Counties, but the livery made a pleasing contrast. As with United Counties, the day of the week made a difference here, as Thames Valley ran extra services on market days on its trunk routes to High Wycombe and Windsor.

In fact, despite the Road Traffic Act and its avowal to cut out 'wasteful competition', you could travel by bus from Windsor to Aylesbury by London Transport or Thames Valley, and, if using the former, by a variety of different ways. Shades of today . . ?

Spectacular livery

My favourite, however, was none of these. To someone born and brought up in Lancashire, an AEC was

something of a novelty. Take a whole fleet of AECs, keep them superbly maintained, and paint them in the most ornate livery imaginable, and you get The City of Oxford Motor Services Ltd whose buses captured my imagination from the start. The livery was spectacular: dark red with maroon contrasting areas, black wings and the so-called 'duck-egg blue' waistrail. It has been illustrated and praised enough, and for me the National Bus Company deserved to die if only for abolishing this visual delight. The second Oxford bus I saw carried my own initials on its registration plate, which was certainly a plus point(!) and what about the destination blinds, carrying, perhaps uniquely, the word 'To'? 'To Thame, via Cuddington, Chearsley, Long Crendon' said the 81 elegantly. Alas, the use of this refined style was to die out as newer buses with

Icknield Coaches of Tring operated this impressive rear-engined Foden with Metalcraft C41C body in a beige and maroon livery. The sun visor is reminiscent of those popular on cars of the period.
R. H. G. Simpson

smaller blinds entered service and via points were omitted, but it seemed fitting for buses from a City renowned, amongst other things, for its English dictionaries.

City of Oxford maintained a small garage in Aylesbury, now built over, and in it were kept amongst other things Regal III halfcabs which spent their last days running the inevitable market-day services to surrounding villages. The company also had a curious habit of parking vehicles on long layover not in its garage but scattered around various side-streets. It certainly made photography simpler, once you had located the side-streets in question – no passengers in the way of the lens! Today all has changed beyond recognition, but for some years it was my delight to make regular trips by bike to see the latest happenings. It was noticeable, for example, that City of Oxford always sent an example or two of their newest vehicles to work the 82 Oxford-Aylesbury service and a glance at the Fleet Developments column in *Buses Illustrated* would give a clue as to what might be expected to turn up. Another point of note was that Red Rover, also an AEC fan, would tend to follow City of Oxford's lead. For example, when the big operator acquired 36ft Reliances with BET Federation bodies, Red Rover got one. When Oxford turned to the Swift, Red Rover followed suit.

One summer's day in 1964, my pal and I decided to be a bit more adventurous in our bus-spottings by bike and having exhausted the delights of Aylesbury, pushed on up the A41 to Bicester, where there was known to be another City of Oxford garage. This turned out to be a big mistake, because for miles there wasn't a thing of interest to be seen, the only break in the monotony being a solitary Thames Trader/Duple Trooper owned by one Murray Saunders of Waddesdon. This coach would be of more value today for its registration number, 8 JNM, than for itself. Other than this, every village seemed without public transport, no bus services used this main highway and when we finally arrived at Bicester the City of Oxford garage housed only a couple of cars and one single-decker. Just outside the town was the depot of Grayline Coaches, a more fruitful place to visit housing a couple of OBs and a rebodied OWB, sundry SB coaches, a newish VAL and an imposing Harrington-bodied Leyland Royal Tiger. Was it worth cycling all that way to see them? Well, no, not really, especially as my pal, who was even then becoming addicted to nicotine, lacked the stamina to cycle back again at anything like a reasonable pace. It took us ages to get back to civilisation, recognisable by the rear end of a Green Line RF waiting to depart from Aylesbury on its long run to Westerham (wherever that was). The 64-mile round trip we did that day remains my all-time daily record for a cycle journey, but I continued to cycle to Aylesbury until I became 'motorised' in 1966. **CB**

New in the spring of 1962 was Red Rover's 27 WKX, which unlike its stable-mate, had a rear entrance. This bus gave many years' service before being exported to Ireland.
R. H. G. Simpson

Bus Routes Serving Aylesbury in the early 1960s

1 LONDON TRANSPORT

301	Aylesbury-Watford
359	Aylesbury-Amersham (joint with United Counties)
706	Aylesbury-Westerham
707	Aylesbury-Oxted

2 UNITED COUNTIES

16	Aylesbury-Luton
141	Aylesbury-St Ives
346	Aylesbury-Northampton
359	Aylesbury-Amersham (joint with London Transport)
360	Aylesbury-Leighton Buzzard
363	Aylesbury-Tring
364	Aylesbury-Cheddington
366	Aylesbury-Halton Camp (from which 365 ran to Tring)
367	Aylesbury-Halton Camp
369	Aylesbury Town Services
386	Stoke Mandeville Hospital-Aylesbury-Newport Pagnell

3 CITY OF OXFORD

81	Aylesbury-Thame
82	Aylesbury-Oxford
82E	Aylesbury-Oxford (express)
83	Aylesbury-Marsh-Kimble Wick
84	Aylesbury-Quainton-Claydon-Bicester
85	Aylesbury-Brill
87	Aylesbury-Dinton-Ford
98	Aylesbury-Grendon Underwood-Bicester
106	Aylesbury-Ludgershall-Bicester

NB: Only 81, 82 and 98 had regular daily services, the remainder being market-day services only.

4 THAMES VALLEY

20/A	Aylesbury-High Wycombe-Windsor
80	Aylesbury-Princes Risborough-High Wycombe

5 RED ROVER

Aylesbury-Buckingham

Aylesbury-Grendon Underwood-Edgcott

Aylesbury Town Services

Born: 27 February 1908

Father: William Austen, manager of fledgling bus company which hired a steam-powered Darracq-Serpollet and ran the whole shoot from a tobacconists' in Maidstone.

Which he called Maidstone & District?: No. According to transport historian Colin Morris who has studied this and other aspects of the southern England bus scene in fascinating depth, it went under the much less specific name of the Commercial Motor Company. Austen soon expanded the service and replaced the borrowed steam bus with petrol-engined vehicles acquired on the never-never from a local ironworks. Failure to make the necessary repayments led to the buses being repossessed and the business was sold to a new owner in May 1910.

Who was?: Walter Flexman French, one of the region's pioneer busmen who would later help get Southdown off the ground.

And French came up with the succinct English geographical name we know and love so well?: Not at first. The ironworks had called it the Maidstone, Chatham & Gravesend Omnibus Service and French managed to make even that sound brief by calling it the Maidstone, Chatham, Gravesend & District Motor Omnibus Service. Just think what would have happened had he thought of adding Tonbridge, Tunbridge Wells, Hildenborough and a few other forms of propulsion to the company's remit at that stage.

It certainly wasn't a name for the present day. No, but it was a present for a name on a day.

Do explain: French's son George turned 30 on 6 August 1910. Walter French marked the day by handing over day-to-day control of the new company which was finally given its familiar and shortened name the following March. The expanding M&D ran itself on something of a wing, a prayer and a shoestring, keeping its buses busy by running them to London at night as fruit lorries, and organising its affairs from a small wooden cabin which would have passed in its day for the equivalent of the Portakabins used by many late-20th century lean bus companies. Colin Morris says it stashed each day's takings in a wastepaper basket in the shed.

But it wasn't a basket case?: Indeed not. For all the difficulties it faced in its earliest days, M&D was attractive enough to encourage British Electric Traction to buy into the business in June 1913. By 1914, it was running 12 routes with 21 buses and could afford to move to better premises elsewhere in Maidstone. We assume it got itself something more secure than the wicker basket.

And it went on growing?: Yes. Expansion was held back by World War 1, but by 1920 it had raised its share capital – £4,000 on formation – to £120,000. Tilling bought into the business in 1921, making it part of what became the Tilling & BAT empire, and by 1924 the share capital had been raised again to £250,000. The Tilling connection brought, first, Tilling-Stevens buses into the M&D fleet, later AEC-powered Bristols which stayed in favour after Tilling & BAT broke up in 1942 and M&D became a BET

company again. The last K6As were delivered in 1949.

How did it grow?: By its own development of markets and by acquiring other operators in the vicinity. Notable additions were North Kent Motor Services of Dartford in 1920, another BET subsidiary; Chatham & District Traction, replacing trams in the Medway towns in 1930 and retaining its separate identity until 1955; Autocar Services of Tunbridge Wells in 1933; and Hastings Tramways (which ran trolleybuses instead of trams from 1929) in 1935. But these bald facts conceal some odd twists and turns.

Such as?: The formation of London Transport led to some swapping of bus operating interests between those on either side of LT's monopoly area. LT got bits of M&D, including North Kent Motor Services, while Autocar was bought from the London Underground group when the rest of its bus operations passed to LT. And the Hastings trolleybuses brought their own curious complications.

Which were?: They functioned as a separate company until September 1957, when that organisation was wound up, the fleet donned M&D logos and the company prepared for a revolutionary sort of double-deck motorbus replacing them in 1959. To whit, the Leyland Atlantean.

Some pioneering work here?: Yes, M&D was one of the earliest Atlantean customers. Its very first went into service in January 1959, following its appearance – along with three others – at the Earls Court show the previous autumn. But this wasn't M&D's first piece of pioneering.

And that was?: The opening of England's first bus station, at Palace Road, Maidstone in 1922.

M&D's later life?: It became part of the National Bus Company in 1969 and for a time was managed jointly with East Kent; it was sold to its management in 1986, then to British Bus in 1995. Now it's again part of one of the biggest groups in the land and goes by the name of Arriva Kent & Sussex which is probably the most accurate geographical name it's had in its life. Call us old sentimental sticks-in-the-mud if you like, but we much prefer to think of it still as M&D.

ALM

Maidstone & District was a faithful Bristol customer until 1949. This 1945 K6A model had been new with a Duple semi-utility body, but in the 1950s received this Weymann 56-seat body. No DH160 (HKE 868) is seen arriving in Tunbridge Wells on a duty from the Medway Towns.
Michael Dryhurst

AIRPORT 71

Heathrow Airport has always boasted an impressive selection of bus services and vehicles. PHILIP WALLIS describes the 1971 scene

AIRPORTS usually provide plenty of interest for the bus and coach enthusiast. Airline passengers need transport to and from the airport, and the large numbers of people employed in the many facets of running an airport along with its support services, need to get to and from work. Often transport is needed for crews and passengers from terminal buildings to the airside.

Bus and coach operators can meet many of these requirements, often with a combination of commercial bus and coach services together with links which may be supported financially by either airlines or the airport authority.

London's Heathrow Airport has always provided good variety in terms of the buses and coaches serving it. I visited Heathrow on what turned out to be two wet Sundays in May and November 1971 in order to observe and photograph the services and vehicles at the airport. At the time I lived near Reading so on

both occasions travelled to and from Heathrow from Reading General station on Thames Valley's Railair Link service (route letter H) riding on Bristol RE coaches. The day return fare was £1.25 in the year that decimal currency had been introduced into the country.

Early Railair links

Perception of the potential for enhanced integrated travel to Heathrow had been recognised in the early 1960s and had been spearheaded by coach operator Charles Rickards (Tours) Ltd which at that time was owned by British Eagle International Airlines. Presumably Rickards' close connection with an airline and airport activity gave it an edge which led to the introduction of Heathrow's first Railair Link coach service in 1963 to High Wycombe station. Planned in co-ordination with British Railways, train connections were provided to the Midlands. Other Railair Link

BOAC's Bedford J4A2 trailer unit with BTC/Samlesbury articulated trailer 212 BLR had been delivered new to the Ministry of Aviation in 1961. It is seen passing through Heathrow in November 1971. All photos by P. R. Wallis

Thames Valley employed Bristol RELH6Gs with Duple Commander II 49-seat coachwork on its Reading to Heathrow Railair Link. No C427 (RJB 427F) is seen outside Terminal 3 in the company of a Rolls-Royce.

Photographed only one month after entering service, Whytes (Edgware) Ford R192 No 13 (URO 843J) fitted with Willowbrook standee bodywork is seen working the Heathrow-Feltham Railair Link in May 1971.

services followed linking Heathrow with Luton, Slough, Watford Junction and Woking stations.

The Slough link had been superseded in March 1967 by a fresh Railair Link to Reading General station which offered more comprehensive connectional facilities than Slough. From Reading, onward travel by train was possible to Wales, the West Country and West Midlands. The contract for this new Railair link was awarded to Tilling group operator Thames Valley despite stiff competition from Rickards. Thames Valley opened up its service using four new Duple Viceroy-boded Bedford VAM14s which in 1968 has been

superseded by a more traditional chassis (for a Tilling company) in the form of four Bristol RELH6Gs with Duple Commander II coachwork.

A further Railair Link was provided by Whytes (Edgware) to nearby Feltham station which offered rail connection with the southwest London suburban network as well as to stations on the Reading-Waterloo line. Whytes used modern 33ft Ford R192s delivered in 1970/71 most of which were fitted with Willowbrook bodywork to standee configuration, briefly fashionable at that period, offering a large standing area but only 29 seats.

Rickards continued to operate the Woking Railair Link using Plaxton Panorama-bodied Leyland Leopards.

If you wanted to get from Heathrow to Central London in those days, there were several choices.

1. The nationalised airlines

In 1966 British European Airways (BEA) had introduced the first of a fleet of 65 AEC/Park Royal Routemaster double-deck coaches linking the West London Air Terminal in Kensington with Heathrow. Since 1947 BEA had contracted out the operation of its London coach service to London Transport who worked the Routemasters from the former tram depot at Chiswick.

An unusual feature of the BEA Routemaster operation was the use of towed baggage trailers; 88 of these trailers had been built by bodybuilder Marshall

Hall's Coaches used Plaxton Panorama-bodied AEC Reliances in a dedicated livery on its Pan-Am contract work such as VYH 55G seen departing Terminal 3 with passengers on board who had just arrived from New York.

Hard Graft! The driver of Hall's Coaches Leyland Atlantean PDR2/1, VYH 46G, on the TWA contract helps a loader to transfer baggage from lorry to coach at Terminal 3.

of Cambridge, the excess in number of trailers over coaches allowed for a 'float' at either terminal. On journeys for domestic flights the trailers were uncoupled at Heathrow and towed to the airside by a BEA Land Rover. At the West London Air Terminal the trailers were shunted by small electric tractor units.

London Transport also operated on BEA's behalf eight Willowbrook-bodied AEC Reliances branded 'Executive Express'. These offered direct airside to West London Air Terminal transfer for the benefit of passengers with hand baggage only on domestic flights.

British Overseas Airways Corporation (BOAC) operated intercontinental flights. BOAC's London

Airways Terminal was located in Victoria's Buckingham Palace Road, coincidentally close to Victoria Coach Station.

During the daily flight peak period, 07.00 to 15.00hrs, BOAC aimed for a five-minute frequency coach service from its London terminal to Heathrow, thereafter reverting to one coach per flight departure. The service was principally provided by 15 MCW-bodied Leyland Atlantean PDR1/1s delivered in 1966, together with six of the larger 33ft Atlantean PDR2/1 model fitted with Roe bodywork received in 1971. The Atlanteans were supplemented by 36ft Ford 676E coaches with Duple Marauder bodywork which during

1971 were progressively replaced by Plaxton-bodied Leyland Leopards. BOAC did not share BEA's enthusiasm for towed bagged trailers. On the Atlantean, passengers' baggage was stowed in a large 290cu ft luggage space on the lower deck serviced by entrance doors on both nearside and offside with the facility for loaders to walk into the bus.

As well as providing travel facilities from central London to Heathrow for its own passengers, BOAC also carried passengers for a number of other world airlines including Air Canada, Air India and Qantas.

2. The American airlines

American airlines Pan-American (Pan-Am) and Trans World Airways (TWA) both subcontracted operation of their central London transfer services to Hall's Coaches of Hounslow which painted coaches used on such work in the livery of the appropriate airline. Around 15 single-deck coaches were used on the Pan-Am contract, typically 36ft AEC Reliances with Plaxton Panorama coachwork. Six coaches were used on the TWA contract, the most interesting of which were three 1969 33ft Leyland Atlantean PDR2/1s whose Roe bodywork, in a similar manner to BOAC's Atlanteans, incorporated a large luggage space at the rear of the lower deck.

3. Airbus Direct – 1970s version

Another Rickards initiative, introduced in 1970, was the provision of a daily coach transfer service from

London Transport No MBS564 (AML 564H) was one of five 1969 AEC Merlins modified for use on Air Express route A1. Alterations included the provision of a split entrance and automatic fare collection equipment. Their dual door Metro-Cammell bodywork accommodated 32 seated and up to 34 standing passengers, some of whom are seen practising at Heathrow Central bus station in May 1971 until the driver feels able to let them aboard.

London Country No RC5 (CUV 63C) is seen leaving Heathrow Central bus station in November 1971 shortly after an allocation of RC class had been made to route 727. These 14 Willowbrook-bodied 36ft long AEC Reliances had a chequered history with LT and London Country, most of them finally being relegated to bus work.

Heathrow direct to a number of central London hotels. This service was worked by a fleet of 15 small Plaxton-bodied Bedford J2 coaches.

Rickards, which in 1967 had been purchased from British Eagle by London coach operator Frames Tours, also undertook contract transfer work for a number of airlines including Aer Lingus, Aerolineas Argentinas, Loftleidir Airways and United Arab Airlines.

London Transport

Ordinary bus services to Heathrow were the sole preserve of London Transport and offered facilities to selected parts of the Greater London area.

Route 82, introduced in September 1970, had replaced the previous route 81B between Hounslow and Heathrow Central from where it was extended on weekdays via the Freight Tunnel thereby providing the first ever bus link to the Cargo Terminal Area and

thence to its terminal at Hatton Cross. The 82 was worked by one-man operated SMS type AEC Swifts.

The longest LT route from Heathrow was the 140 worked by RT type AEC Regent IIIs, which covered considerable tracts of London's northwestern suburbs, before terminating at Mill Hill Broadway.

Route 223 was one-man operated using RF type AEC Regal IVs linking the airport with Uxbridge and Ruislip.

Route 285 provided links to the suburbs to the south of Heathrow en route to Kingston-upon-Thames. The 285 had recently been converted, in March 1971, to one-man operation with SMS type AEC Swifts.

There were no underground links to Heathrow in 1971 at which time the Piccadilly line terminated at Hounslow West. Connection thence to Heathrow Central were provided by LT Air Express Route A1 worked by one-man operated MBS class AEC Merlins.

London Country

London Country, as successors to the former London Transport Country Area, operated Green Line route 727 which in entirety linked Luton Airport with Crawley travelling via both Heathrow and Gatwick airports. The 727 had been introduced by LT in 1967 in a determined attempt to build-up radial Green Line services. When introduced, the 74-mile long route was the longest in the Green Line network. By 1971 the route was worked by a mixture of RF class AEC Regal IV coaches which had been 'modernised' in 1966/7 and coaches from the 1965 RC class of 36ft AEC Reliance with Willowbrook coachwork.

Internal transfer services

Internal transfers of both flight crews and passengers from airside to the terminal buildings were the responsibilities of BEA and BOAC. A variety of buses and coaches were used on these duties, the most unusual of which were Bedford J4A2 tractor units which pulled articulated British Trailer Company/Samlesbury 44-seat trailer units with central entrances on both nearside and offside. These units had been inherited by both the airlines from the Ministry of Aviation on 1 April 1962 when responsibility for the transfer work had passed from the ministry to the airlines.

More modern vehicles in use on transfer duties included a number of twin-steer Bedford VAL14s, with Marshall bodywork in service with BEA and Duple (Midland) 12-seat Bedford J2s, with BOAC.

The inter-terminal passenger transfer service was provided by Hall's Coaches whose operations had expanded dramatically from only eight coaches owned in 1965 to around 100 by 1971.

This phenomenal growth was founded largely on increased airport work including the Pan-Am and TWA contracts already mentioned, combined with Hall's acquisition of West London coach operator Valliant-Cronshaw.

Hall's used a variety of secondhand AEC Reliances in Valliant-Cronshaw livery, on the inter-terminal transfer service along with a number of former Southern/Western National ECW bus-bodied Bristol LS5G saloons.

Above: **BEA's No C569 (OYF 269F) was one of 10 twin-steer Bedford VAL14s with 40-seat Marshall bodywork introduced in 1967 for crew and airside transfer duties. Still displaying old fleet number 6569 the bus passes along the main thoroughfare at Heathrow.**

Left: **In Valliant-Cronshaw livery is Hall's Coaches AEC Reliance 446 CWK in use on inter-terminal transfer duties in May 1971.**

In 1970 the British Airports Authority had sponsored an internal service for employees at the airport covering a 3½-mile circular route to a four-minute headway. The contractor for the service was Whytes (Edgware), also operators of the Feltham Railair Link already referred to, using the same Willowbrook-bodied Ford R192 standee buses.

Hotel courtesy coaches

A number of hotels in the proximity of Heathrow offered direct coach transfer facilities from hotel to airport and *vice versa*. In most cases the coach operation was contracted out to one of the local coach concerns.

The benefit of hindsight

Looking back to the Heathrow bus and coach scene in 1971, central London was understandably the main traffic objective. With the absence of any form of direct rail link perforce journeys involved road travel, except perhaps for the select few who had access to helicopters. The various airlines offered high frequency services to their central London terminals. The traveller also had the option of Airbus Express A1 to Hounslow West and then the Piccadilly Line, probably most useful for intermediate destinations. Then there was Rickard direct service to certain hotels.

Present-day London United Airbus routes A1 and A2 have superseded the former airlines services,

Former Western National ECW-bodied Bristol LS5G, MOD 964, is seen in use with Hall's Coaches on inter-terminal transfer duties outside Terminal 2 in November 1971.

offering a choice of boarding points in central London compared to the one central terminal point of the former airlines' services. Rickards direct service to Central London hotels anticipated today's Airbus Direct facility by some 25 years.

The Piccadilly Line finally became operational from Heathrow in December 1977, and in 1998 the Heathrow Express direct rail service was introduced between Heathrow to Paddington with a journey time of just 15min.

London Transport's bus services to certain parts of suburban London were arguably just about adequate in 1971 but certainly not comprehensive. The 140 (in truncated form with terminus at Harrow Weald) and 285 are still serving Heathrow today, perhaps best regarded as the framework upon which a much more comprehensive network has since been built.

Pointers for future trends in the development of public transport to Heathrow were to be found in the early Railair Link services which recognised the concept of passengers' (they weren't called customers in those days) convenience whilst starting to address, perhaps not deliberately at the time, the problem of

car movements at the airport. The Reading Railair Link has gone from strength to strength, as also has the Woking Railair Link now with Speedlink Airport Services.

Green Line 727 was another mould-breaker when initiated by LT in 1967. It was the first coach service to serve Heathrow from radial points to both north and south and was a recognition, along with the Railair Links, that a direct facility might appeal more to passengers than forced connectional journeys, often via central London. The 727 also provided the first coach link between three of London's principal airports Gatwick, Heathrow and Luton.

This concept has been extensively developed in the years since, helped by extensive motorway construction particularly the M25. Radial coach services, provided by Speedlink and others, are available to destinations as diverse as Brighton or Norwich. A virtual shuttle service of coaches plies the M25 between Heathrow and Gatwick.

Noticeably absent from Heathrow Central in 1971 were any all-year round long distance express services . . . despite the fact that Associated Motorways Bristol 'Greyhound' coach services and the extensive Royal Blue network passed close to the airport on either the M4 or Great West Road on their westerly approaches to London.

Likewise Green Line routes 704/5 (Windsor-Sevenoaks/Tunbridge Wells via Central London)

In 1971 non-British built coaches were rare in this country. Mercedes-Benz 0302 GMC 748J is surveyed by the law as it passes Terminal 3 in November 1971 offering opulent conveyance for the patrons of the Skyline Hotel.

working to a combined 30-min headway with Routemaster coaches as well as Thames Valley's hourly frequency double-deck operated route B (Reading-London) passed along the Bath Road on Heathrow's northern perimeter but did not enter Heathrow Central. Any passengers for that destination had to change to LT red Central Area buses at 'Heathrow Airport North'.

Nowadays, Heathrow has become a major traffic objective for National Express coaches from all parts of the country as well as other operators.

Surprising too in 1971 was the complete lack of bus service provision to high population centres to the southwest of the airport such as Staines or towns in northwest Surrey which were all well within the airport's employment catchment area. Nowadays such areas are well served by bus services which extend even further into the counties to the west of Heathrow. **CB**

Bibliography

PSV Circle/Omnibus Society Fleet History PN5 'British Airways Board and its predecessors'

MANAGING ON THE RIGHT LINES

GEOFF BURROWS looks at 'tram' managers who left a legacy of fine buses

Glasgow No 629 (BUS 195), seen here in postwar years after refurbishment, has lost its streamlined markings, but none of the other Glasgow features. This was an Albion Venturer CX19 with one of the last Cowieson bodies to be built.
Roy Marshall

WHILE THE title and main objective of this yearbook is the classic bus, there have to be excursions into other modes of transport from time to time to judge the relevant actions of the men in power in the past. In other words, what is it that makes a classic bus stand out from its contemporaries? A point of view that seems to be ignored is that the men who were responsible for the classic trams of the 1930s, were also responsible for the classic buses of the same period.

Ask the average tram enthusiast for a list of the top half-dozen operators and it will probably name Glasgow, Leeds, Sheffield, London, Blackpool and Sunderland amongst them. If you ask the average bus enthusiast for a list of 1930s municipal favourites, it will probably include some or all of the same names. This is no coincidence, because on closer study it

becomes clear that what makes a good transport manager is not his choice of modes, but his ability to produce a design or specification for both modes which will result in a high-profile, comfortable vehicle in which the public will enjoy travelling. He will also design and develop his services to achieve the maximum revenue while ensuring that the trams and buses are complementary to each other, thus ensuring the maximum number of passengers on both types of vehicle. In fact a lot of the pioneering work in

developing the image of the modern bus was actually done by men who are more popularly known as tram operators, and their real influence on the bus industry is largely ignored.

If we look first of all at a name which is not on our lists at all, you may begin to understand. When Ronald Fearnley became manager at Coventry in 1933, one of the first things that he looked at was a programme to abandon the city tramway system. He also had as a very high priority the improvement of the appearance of those trams while he had to continue running them. Thus when the new image of the Coventry bus fleet emerged, with the Daimler COA6/Brush design as its standard, the startlingly simple but very effective livery changes, combined with the use of bold and clear sans-serif lettering and numbering was applied to the trams

Restrained streamlining was developed for Sunderland's buses, with the 'SCT' indicator on the offside balancing the nearside destination indicator. No 48 (GR 5219) is seen before delivery in 1938.
Roy Marshall/ East Pennine

Seen here in postwar years, Sunderland No 52 (GR 6075) has kept its streamline livery but lost the distinctive diamonds which bore the coat of arms. Perhaps they have been washed away by the Tide!
Roy Marshall/ East Pennine

as well. So while the new buses were appearing in ever larger numbers, the remaining trams were not, as in so many places, left to be run into the ground. They were maintained and, in many cases improved, because Fearnley knew that to lose a tram passenger was to lose a future bus passenger.

Royal Commission

A Royal Commission to investigate and discuss the state of transport in this country was appointed by the government of the day and in 1930 this Commission reported back. It expressed the opinion that no new tramways should be built and those that existed should be allowed to disappear. So it was a somewhat shocked council in 1933 Blackpool that heard the report of the newly appointed manager, Walter Luff, in which he recommended not the scrapping but the retention and modernisation of the trams in that famous resort. Now this often-repeated fact is well known to transport historians. What seems to get forgotten is the fact that parallel to the introduction of the modern trams was a new design of bus for the town. This bore all the luxury features of the new trams, including centre entrances for quick and easy loading, comfortable moquette-covered seats, and decorative ceilings and lamps. This specification included the fitting of full fronts on the

Blackpool No 147 (FV 8989), a 1937 Leyland TD4 with locally-built Burlingham bodywork to Blackpool requirements, has more than a passing resemblance to the modern tram fleet, but also to the contemporary Sunderland buses.
G. Burrows collection

buses emphasising the streamline fashion of the era. Luff also took pains to ensure that the local coachbuilder, H. V. Burlingham was fully involved in the design of the buses, and so to that company went most of the orders, thus ensuring local employment.

It is true to say that centre-entrance trams and buses were not invented in Blackpool. It is also true that modern designs were appearing elsewhere. However, it was Blackpool that became the first operator to become totally committed to centre-entrance trams and buses, with a common image. Streamlining too, with various arrangements of swoops and curves in unlikely places, became the vogue, but it was in Blackpool that the first fully acceptable image of streamlined trams and buses appeared, and this was achieved largely with straight lines! The few curves that were used had the subtle refinements of well-balanced design. All this, with a new livery of cream and green, achieved the modern, attractive look which many envied. The Walter Luff philosophy was modern *transport*, not just modern *tramways*.

Charles Hopkins, Luff's contemporary at Sunderland, was another manager regarded as a 'tram man', but who in fact did more for the image of the modern bus that most. Hopkins started the Sunderland bus fleet with a batch of Leyland single-deckers, by the end of the 1930s he had placed in service nearly 30 double-deck centre-entrance Daimler COG5s. In Sunderland the modernisation evolved gradually, going from a sedate livery of brown waist panels with cream above, to an attractive red with layers of cream, finally emerging in an attractive style of red with cream flashes. Hopkins' trams, on the other hand, are what brought him his fame. First his rebuilds of old cars into fast fully-enclosed machines, then his many purchases of secondhand cars which he proceeded to improve out of all recognition, and last but not least his new cars for the town, culminating in centre-entrance streamliners not unlike Blackpool's.

Total commitment

Here was a working tramway system, serving the public, making money, but fully integrated into a modern bus system which he developed as part of a total commitment to carrying the people of Sunderland about their business and pleasure. Yet it was the standard of the bus fleet of Sunderland which raised the town transport well beyond its contemporaries. Comfortable, luxurious, reliable, frequent, the adjectives positively stream out. Not for Sunderland shipyards a line of tired old buses to return home in after work, but comfortable and pleasant modern machines (apart from the smoke, of course, for the northerners liked their tobacco, and the windows tightly closed against the wind). The football

crowds too, were shifted by these same buses, their ability to radiate in straight lines from Roker Park gave them that distinct advantage over the trams, which relied on their high capacity to do their part in moving the football fans along the fixed routes which of course all radiated from the town centre, some distance away. I suppose that few people today realise that Sunderland in the 1930s was not just a shipbuilding town, it was a seaside resort as well. People came for day trips, and for many it was the place for the annual holiday. Roker and Seaburn were famous for their

miles of beaches, bands in the parks and the autumn illuminations. So Hopkins had decided that the standard of the vehicles had to be high. It was indeed a pleasure after a day at work or a night at the theatre to enjoy the comfort of a Sunderland tram or bus for the journey home. As we have seen, the bus system began under his management and grew to eight regular bus services and many specials serving all parts of the town by 1940.

Glasgow, with over a thousand trams, was one of the last bastions of tramways in the British Isles. Yet in

Sheffield got what it wanted on this batch of AEC Regents in 1940 by building the bodies in its own workshops. Note the raised waistrail, double sliding windows and protruding radiator, the latter to house the 8.8-litre engine.
Roy Marshall

1935, most of the fleet was over 20 years old. The management philosophy was to keep the trams, literally. Not by just make do and mend, though to the outsider that's how it looked, but by maintaining a rolling programme of modernisation of the cars. This meant that while they looked every day of their age, they had received top deck covers, vestibules, bow collectors, high speed motors, air brakes and roller bearing axles.

Meanwhile in only 11 years from 1924 and the start of bus operations, over 600 buses had been acquired and by the date that we are talking about had achieved a recognised 'Glasgow' look. There was already a luxurious feel to the buses with polished wood finishes, comfortable moquette and leather on the seats, decorated ceilings and lamps. It is worth noting that all these items, which were subsequently featured on the 'Coronation' trams, were used first on Glasgow buses.

Local industry

For the buses once again local industry was involved, in this case F. D. Cowieson Ltd, the Glasgow coachbuilder which until 1938 built the majority of the corporation bus bodies. An attractive 'house style' was developed, the general outline was not unlike the contemporary Leyland bodywork, with a number of purely Glasgow features, making them instantly recognisable, even in black and white photographs. For the 1937/8 deliveries, Weymann were also involved for the first time, with a particularly distinctive version of its very attractive bodywork.

Unfortunately for various reasons Albion Motors did not – and never did – achieve more than a very

small share of the chassis orders. Some day someone may write a definitive history of that company and we may then find out the reasons. Be that as it may, it did supply a number of chassis to the Glasgow requirement, and these ran successfully for many years. These included Glasgow's first diesel-engined buses, powered by Gardner 6LW engines. However, the lion's share of orders always went to AEC and Leyland, and some of the 1937 requirement went to Daimler, which were at the time achieving many successful sales in the municipal sector.

When it was decided that Glasgow was to be the venue of the 1938 British Empire Exhibition, the corporation looked at the possible numbers of visitors expected. To cater for these, 100 trams of a new design were ordered, and 100 buses. These large bogie trams with all the modern technical features developed for the existing fleet were to be fully streamlined, and the interiors were to include all the comfort and style of the corporation buses. By the time of the opening of the Empire Exhibition in May 1938, 39 of the 'Coronation' trams had been received, and 65 of the buses. During the period 1936-40 the corporation built and placed in service 153 new trams; in the same period they placed in service 400 new buses. The foremost tramway

NIVES.

No 335 (EWA 535) was built in 1937 by local bodybuilder Cravens on a Leyland TD5c chassis for Sheffield. The luxurious interior is not revealed by the business-like exterior.
Roy Marshall

operator it certainly was, but by now it was very definitely one of the foremost bus operators as well.

Gradually modernised

In Sheffield they did things differently. The tramcar fleet was not modernised progressively, but replaced progressively, so that not only the technology but the appearance was gradually modernised. Both residents and visitors in Sheffield were not aware of any sharp change of image as in Glasgow between the 'Standards' and the 'Coronations', but the result was every bit as modern and luxurious as that city's newest. The bus fleet too was progressively improved in specification and detail, with one of the most comprehensively-equipped depots in this country to service and maintain it. However, the most significant developments were to the route network, for the railway companies had a joint share in these activities. The bus services were expanded carefully and completely so that as far as possible they did not compete with trams, but were complementary to them. This was not easy, especially in a city which is built into a series of valleys, which thus restricts the numbers of possible roads and routes anyway. That this was successfully done is apparent not only by the growing bus fleet, but also the number of new trams that were built every year to maintain the low age profile of the fleet and the numbers of cars in it.

The Sheffield bus fleet was in many ways a mirror of

the tram fleet. Buses were replaced on a regular basis, utilising the best in current technology and acceptability. The general manager during these formative years was Arthur Fearnley (yes, father of Ronald), and he was one of the first to specify large capacity double-deckers, and also diesel engines, automatic and semi-automatic transmissions, and large, simple, easily-understood destination displays. The bus interiors were bright, clean, neat and uncluttered with different seating colours on each deck. The exteriors were in startling contrast to the gloom in the steelworking heart of the city, being pristine in cream with blue bands, neatly lined out. Not for Sheffield the faint-hearted acceptance of dark colours in dark places, but a loud and clear statement that here were buses to be proud of; work places may be dirty but the buses didn't have to be. Thus Fearnley ensured that the whole image of the transport system was a positive statement of confidence in its ability to move the citizens of the city comfortably and conveniently, on the buses as well as the trams.

The impact of W. Vane Moreland on the image of

Above: *The subtle changes made to the standard Weymann bodies for Sheffield in 1939 are enough to give an entirely different appearance from their standard body. No 7 (FWJ 807) was an 8.8-litre engined AEC Regent II for the jointly owned 'B' fleet.*
G. Burrows collection

Left: *No, not a tram replacement, but a visitor to the National Tramway Museum at Crich on 'Yorkshire Day', this Leeds AEC Regent with Roe body epitomised the bus fleet of that city. Trams may have been the mainstay, but without the vast fleet of comfortable modern buses such as No 139 (ANW 682) city transport would have been run by private operators.*
G. Burrows

the Leeds bus in the 1930s has already been discussed in CB6. The quality of the buses and services in other tram-oriented fleets such as Aberdeen, Edinburgh and Liverpool cannot be ignored. While it is true to say that in many fleets where buses had greater or even total dominance, much work was done to create what would today be called an 'upmarket image', it would seem on reflection that a great deal of the real bus improvement was achieved by so-called 'tram managers'. **CB**

CHECKPOINT

No 2: Bristol LS

Born: Lowestoft, 12 December 1950, the day the first completed example emerged from Eastern Coach Works.

Father: Stanley Kennedy, chairman, British Transport Commission's Tilling Group management committee.

Conceived: Around June 1949, possibly earlier. Like many parents, Kennedy may have been practising for some time before admitting that the LS was on its way. Doubtless, many others were involved in its development, but this is a project the top man was prepared to endorse.

And the letters stood for?: Light Saloon is the received wisdom, which is very much what the LS was, with an unladen weight of a shade over six tons. It was the first of a generation of volume-built lightweight, or lighter-weight underfloor horizontal-engined single-deckers which became the British bus industry's standard fodder throughout the 1950s. It came out shortly after Bristol's even more revolutionary double-decker, the LD, hit the streets. The received wisdom is that LD was an abbreviation of its model name, Lodekka, which just goes to show you can read one L of a lot of meanings into one initial. Or was the Lodekka LD also the Light Decker?

But the LS wasn't the first underfloor-engined saloon?: No. Midland Red, Leyland and AEC can comfortably vie with one another for that accolade. And both Beadle's of Rochester and Sentinel were producing various lighter-weight integrals by then, but those integrals had a limited following, Leyland and AEC were producing some highly durable but rather heavy machines, and Midland Red could only build buses for its own needs.

Could Bristol do any better?: Up to a point. As part of BTC, it wasn't permitted to supply buses on the open market, but the combined might of the Tilling and Scottish Bus Group companies, London Transport and acquired operations such as Red & White and the Balfour Beatty fleets in the east Midlands gave it a potentially attractive – and captive – market to supply.

What made the LS so light?: The combination of a pressed steel underframe and aluminium alloy body in a semi-integral structure which provided maximum strength with a minimum amount of materials. The first prototypes were even lighter as they had aluminium underframes and narrower axles. It was also intended that it would have a new design of lightweight Bristol engine.

Southern National No 1692 (LTA 989) was one of over 100 Bristol LS5G buses delivered to the Western National group in the years 1952-7. All carried bodywork by Eastern Coach Works.
Michael Dryhurst

And that was?: It wasn't anything because it didn't make it into reality. But reliable sources such as Alan Townsin (who else?) say this would have been a four-cylinder of around six-litre capacity. That's a fair description of the infinitely more powerful Euro 3 version of the Cummins B-Series due to make its debut around the same time as you buy this book.

So what powered the LS?: The first LSX prototype (for Bristol Tramways) got what probably was the only Bristol XWA, an experimental version of the six-cylinder, 8.15-litre LSW; this was a horizontal version of the vertical AVW, and it set the standard for the production LS6B. The second prototype (for Eastern Counties and happily preserved today) went into service in June 1951 with a Gardner 4HLW, making it a forerunner of the LS4G, of which Eastern Counties bought the only five. More respectable numbers of LS6Bs went to Crosville, United Auto, United Counties, United Welsh, Southern Vectis and Thames Valley, but most of the eventual run of over 1,400 got Gardner engines.

And those weren't 4HLWs?: No. Most buses got 5HLWs, while coaches and some buses – including Mansfield District, Midland General, United Welsh, Thames Valley, Wilts & Dorset and Alexander examples – had 6HLWs. There also were such experimental oddities as a pair with Commer two-strokes (LS3C would be their logical description) and one for Bristol Omnibus with an AEC engine – the only theoretical LS6A.

What about their bodies?: Bus and dual purpose versions, which accounted for two thirds of all Bristol LSs, changed little. The 1950 prototypes' downswept windscreens weren't perpetuated in production and the back windows were made more shallow to accommodate rear destination displays where operators still specified them. While most sat no more than 45, Lincolnshire Road Car and United Welsh each got an experimental 54-seater in 1954, with three-and-two seating crammed in and the emergency exit relocated in the centre of the back end. There was a bigger change in coach design after the first 105 LS coaches were built in 1952/3. Originally, they had quarterlights and a windscreen that was supposed to wind down like a car's side windows, only it didn't do that very well. It was replaced by a hinged opening windscreen and the quarterlights were abandoned.

And ECW bodied the lot?: Almost. While Scottish Omnibuses and Alexander took 70 ECW-bodied LS6Gs, Western SMT, which exercised some considerable strength in getting the buses it wanted, persuaded BTC to have its only 19 LSs bodied by Alexander and went on to get rather more Alexander-bodied MWs when the LS was replaced in 1958. ECW made up for this by fitting LS bodies on small batches of Leyland Royal Tigers, AEC Regal IVs and a Guy Arab LUF for English fleets. London Transport, by the way, did evaluate an LS5G in Green Line colours, but it wasn't in the market for this size of bus.

So who bought the most LSs?: United Auto. Along with its Durham District associate, United owned 290 LS5Gs and 45 LS6Bs. It got the first production LS5G buses in 1952 and the last production LSs, LS6B coaches, in 1958. Western National/Southern National had over 200, including some impressive Royal Blue coaches, and Bristol Omnibus ran over 100. Bristol even had a few refurbished in the mid-1970s with fancy new window rubbers and LH-style windscreens.

ALM

VINTAGE '58

As MICHAEL DRYHURST recounts 1958 was not a good year for Chateau Broadway, bin 55

On 22 January 1958 the last of the prototype Routemasters entered service. This was RML3, the Weymann version which was powered with the Leyland O.600 engine and running units. Careful study of this and CRL4 (on the next page) will show many subtle differences in the frontal treatment around the bonnet and wings.
All black-and-white photos by Michael Dryhurst

JUST OVER 40 years ago London Transport attained its Silver Jubilee but there was little to celebrate, in that 1958 brought nothing but anguish and heartache to the LTE and its staff and the year marked a turning-point in London Transport's history.

LT's 1958 started normally enough, with a few route changes being introduced on 8 January, the most notable of these being route 252, Romford station to Birch Road; the route was extended from the latter point to Collier Row and in line with the then-standard LT practice for lightly-trafficked routes, the frequency was reduced while capacity was increased by way of (bureaucratic) compensation. This was achieved by replacing the 31-seat Leyland Tiger PS1 with an equal number of the RT double-decker.

Towards the end of January a new agreement was reached between the LTE and Southdown concerning running rights within Crawley New Town; hitherto, the boundary agreement designated the north of the town as LT territory, the south side of Crawley to SMS. The new agreement provided for each operator to serve any part of the town, within a pre-agreed mileage allowance, the immediate effect being the withdrawal

Top: *The end of January 1958 saw a revised agreement between LTE and Southdown concerning running rights within Crawley New Town, permitting each operator into areas hitherto 'off-limits'. One immediate effect was the extension of Southdown 23/23A into the Northgate area. Southdown No 790, an East Lancs-bodied Leyland Titan PD2/12, ventures beyond Crawley bus station, the former terminus of route 23. On the right, LTE RF106 has a route-identity crisis; at the time the Green Line route out of Crawley was the 710 – so why is it showing '709 London' on its blind?*

Above: *On 8 January 1958 the ECW Routemaster, CRL4, took up duty on the lengthy Green Line route 711, on which it is seen here laying over at High Wycombe (HE) garage. In this view the upstairs luggage racks can be clearly seen.*

Right: *Many of the RT class sold in 1958 were snapped up by Scottish operators. Seen leaving Renfrew Ferry is No 25 in the fleet of Cunningham's Bus Service – ostensibly a 1947 RT but obviously carrying a much newer body . . .*

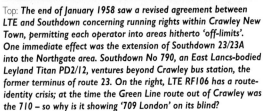

of LT route 483, bus station to Northgate, and replacing it with an extension of the SMS Brighton-Crawley 23 over the 483 road to Northgate, and the introduction of SMS 23A, Northgate-Pease Pottage.

Early in January 1958, RML3, the Weymann Routemaster with Leyland powertrain, went to Willesden garage for training and entered service on route 8 on 22 January; likewise, the Eastern Coach Works Routemaster (Leyland-powered) CRL4 went to High Wycombe garage and took up duties on Green Line route 711 from 8 January.

Surplus buses

One of the major LTE developments of 1958 had its origins in 1954 or even earlier . . . On 10 November

Although photographed after 1958, the colour shots show vehicles and routes from the earlier period. Roofbox RT3846 arrives back at its home garage, Norbiton (NB) from work on route 14 in April 1962.

Colour photos by Geoff Rixon

1954 was delivered to London Transport its last RTL, the next day followed its very last RT, but the event was clouded by a minor snag – there wasn't any work for these brand-new buses. The pundits had predicted steady traffic growth whereas the reality was declining traffic resulting in service reductions, and although it had been foreseen that there would be a surplus of new buses, with an attendant reduction in the new vehicle construction programme, such reduction was both insufficient and tardy, the result being 144 unwanted new buses – 81 green RTs, 63 RTLs. One hesitates to calculate the amount of wasted capital investment as these brand-new vehicles were placed into store immediately, with wheels removed, sitting-up on blocks at Garston and Loughton garages . . . By January 1958, $3\frac{1}{4}$ years later, these same new and unused buses were still in store. At which time LTE had decided finally to place into service these vehicles, this being achieved by withdrawing and offering for sale a like number of older vehicles from within the RT family. The original intention had been that these disposals would be comprised exclusively of the RTL, but when it was realised(!) that the oldest RTLs were younger than the oldest RTs a rethink took place. But still it seemed that the inmates were running the asylum inasmuch as it was decided now that disposal would be on the basis of the oldest-registered vehicles within the RT/RTL classes, a decision that seemingly

overlooked the obvious that when going through an Aldenham overhaul, many of these supposedly 'old' registered buses carried very much more modern bodies (and possibly very much more modern chassis!). Included within the disposals were some significantly-numbered buses; RT402, the first postwar RT to enter service, RTL501, the first Leyland RT into service, and RTL1, numerically the first of the type. These earlier RT buses found ready buyers both in UK independent and municipal fleets, while some 40 RTs and 84 RTLs went to the newly-constituted Ceylon Transport Board.

All of the 63 'new' RTLs had entered service by 25 March while only a number of the RTs had done so, 19 still being in store at the end of 1958.

Mileage cuts

On 30 April 1958 the Central Buses summer programme was introduced, which coincided with the (long-deferred) mileage cuts. The latter had been proposed originally for implementation in the autumn of 1957 but were postponed in deference to staff

objections. However, to comply with a government requirement that fares should be held down as part of an anti-inflation policy, the only way that the Executive could address this was with mileage cuts, despite the deep, and long-held, suspicion by staff that these were *job* cuts, and the plan was vociferously opposed by the Transport & General Workers Union to such a degree that strike action had been threatened. The LTE plan was for Monday-Friday schedules to be cut by a total of 113 buses, Saturdays 197, although Sundays saw an increase of 319 buses, but this was still 159 less than the equivalent day in 1957 . . . Changes in the wake of this programme saw route 24 losing RT in favour of RTW operation plus alterations to routes 67, 70, 96, 98A, 104, 106, 127, 182, 198 and 226. The changes were initiated speedily; the union response was equally swift. Within six days there was not an LTE bus to be seen in public service . . .

August 1957 had seen the opening of negotiations for a wage increase for all LTE bus crews, proposals being submitted by the workforce to the T&GWU for a substantial wages increase to cover bus operating staff and engineering workers. Over the next nine months, proposals and counter-proposals flew between 55 Broadway and union hq, with a not inconsiderable amount of government pressure also, but with each side

desperately trying to avoid the inevitable, the chasm was just too wide, with the mileage cuts being the proverbial 'last straw', and a total strike started after the last service vehicles ran into their respective garages and depots on the night of Sunday 4 May 1958.

The strike was 100% effective. Pickets were placed at all depots and garages, and not a bus, coach or trolleybus moved, and thus it was for the full seven weeks of the strike. After three weeks of this the industrial commissioner sought to bring together the two sides; even the prime minister intervened, for although both the Underground and the suburban services of British Railways were running full schedules, still the London travelling public was suffering enormous discomfort and inconvenience. But to no avail. Still the chasm between the two sides was as wide as ever, and the major stumbling block was a different application of tactics.

Both sides acknowledged that a prolonged stoppage would affect future demand for bus services; the view of the LTE was that this in itself would deter the union from taking strike action whereas the union stance was that for the very self-same reason, the executive would settle quickly to *avoid* such a situation. With the capital and much of the Home Counties deprived of bus and coach services, as mentioned above the population was forced to endure severe difficulties in travel and in an effort to alleviate this, the executive took the then-unprecedented decision to allow other operators to run services.

Above: *To be seen around the West End of London at the time of the strike was this ex-Aldershot & District Dennis Lance II/East Lancs, by then owned by Margo's of Bexleyheath. It did not appear to operate any scheduled services but it was a very familiar sight; it is seen here one evening in May 1958 emerging from Whitehall into Trafalgar Square.*

Above right: *The Central Area lost some 25% of its lowbridge routes when the Merton-based 127 fell victim to the cuts. RLH70, a 1952-delivered AEC Regent III 9612E with Weymann 53-seat lowbridge body, lays over at Morden station in less-threatened days.*

People's League

First on the scene was the semi-political (and shamelessly right-wing) organisation 'The People's League for the Defence of Freedom', which began operating buses on 31 May, not charging fares in the absence of formal LTE consent; by 13 June this was forthcoming and the League had obtained licenses for the following routes, on which was charged a flat fare of sixpence (2^{1}/2p):

1	Victoria-Marble Arch
2	Addington-Croydon
3	Barnes-Roehampton
5	Archway-Friern Barnet
6	Oval-Thornton Heath
7	Surbiton-Richmond
8	Woolwich-Chislehurst

Licences were granted also for London area services to Camden Coaches, Sevenoaks, Chiltern Queens, Edward Thomas of Ewell, Whitefriars of Wembley and Wright, Harlow. All of these were established operators with a fleet of vehicles to call upon whereas the League was not, and thus hired a real rag-bag mix of vehicles from dealer Cyril Green Enterprises, the

'operating base' being a car park on the north side of Wandsworth Common. This was the 'fleet' of the People's League for the Defence of Freedom:

FT 5702, AEC Regent II/Weymann H56R, ex-Tynemouth
JG 9934/56, Leyland Tiger TS8/Park Royal C32R, ex-East Kent
ABE 335, Leyland Tiger TS8/Harrington C34F, ex-Lincolnshire
BFN 934/9, Leyland Titan TD7/Park Royal H54R, ex-Crosville
BTF 21, Leyland Lion LT7c/Leyland B34F, ex-Lytham St Annes
BTF 28, Leyland Titan TD4c/Leyland FH54R, ex-Lytham St Annes
CFM 61/365, Leyland Titan TD5/ECW L52R, ex-Crosville
CRX 540, Bristol K6A/Strachans L55R, ex-Thames Valley
DBC 221/4, AEC Renown 0664/MCCW H64R, ex-Leicester
DLY 984, Dennis Lancet II/ Duple C35F, ex-Empress, E2
DUC 904, Leyland Tiger TS7D/Beadle B43C, ex-City Coach Co
EWO 475, Bedford OWB/Duple B29F, ex-Red & White
FTC 618, Daimler CWA6/Duple H56R, ex-Lytham St Annes
GCD 688, Leyland Titan TD7/Park Royal H52R, ex-Crosville
HTC 614/5, Crossley SD42/Crossley B36R, ex-Lancaster

From personal recollection the majority of the above buses ran in the livery of their former operator, and although providing a wonderful sight for the enthusiast, their presence was no panacea but more of a gesture more likely to inflame the impasse, which may well have been the intention of the League, anyway . . .

Return to work

Eventually, on 20 June, the strike was settled with a smooth return to work on the 21st. Nobody had won. Not LTE, not the T&GWU and certainly not the public, especially as now a much-depleted service was operated because staff shortages had been compounded by the strike; during the stoppage many staff had left for other work, none of whom had been replaced because recruitment and training had been at a complete standstill.

Late June saw the mileage-cuts programme applied to the trolleybus services with cuts of 36 buses Monday-Friday, 28 on Saturdays and 50 on Sundays. It was, of course, this very programme which was one of the root causes of the strike. Other trolleybus happenings were the July opening of Butterwick, part of the

Hammersmith gyratory system; the new overhead across Hammersmith Broadway and along Butterwick was the last occasion on which new trolleybus wiring in London was authorised by an Act of Parliament.

It was but a short period of time before the devastating effects of the strike were assessed, and action was both draconian and swift. On 20 August, 19 routes were withdrawn completely:

4A	Finsbury Park-Clapham Common
7	Acton-Liverpool Street
17	London Bridge-Park Royal
26	Ilford-Lambourne End
48	Cannon Street-West Norwood
50A	Embankment-Brixton Garage
60	Colindale-Old Ford
67	Waterloo-Stoke Newington
86	Chadwell Heath-Brentwood
96	Putney Common-Redbridge
127	Morden-St Helier (lowbridge route)
149	Grove Park-Cannon Street
169	Clapham Junction-Victoria
189	Cannon Street-North Cheam
238	Emerson Park-Noak Hill
239	Gidea Park-Romford
249	Corbets Tey-Upminster Park Estate
251A	North Finchley-Amos Grove

Above: *RTW13 at Camden Town on route 74 in August 1965.*

Opposite top: *In September 1958 the Historic Commercial Vehicle Society held its second rally of the year, at the Southall works of AEC. One of the exhibits was RM2, having received a new 9.6-litre AV590 engine in place of its 7.7-litre AV470, plus Central Area livery.*

Opposite below: *Still with its original front end styling, Green Line Routemaster prototype, by this time renumbered RMC4, at Addlestone garage on route 716 in April 1962.*

Below: *Saunders-bodied roofbox RT1536 pulls away from traffic lights on the Edgware Road in May 1962 alongside a Valliant, Ealing AEC Reliance/Plaxton coach.*

The 260 was cut-back from Colindale to operate Cricklewood-Surrey Docks, and later cuts planned for the complete withdrawal of the 123, 193, 664, 683, 695 with partial withdrawal of 18B, 25, 33, 39 and 83. The Country Area had seen service revisions on 23 July, to address 'a drop in passenger traffic and to reduce operating costs'. The Central Area cuts saw a Mon-Fri reduction of 175 double-deckers, 125 on Sats, but only 18 on Suns. In October, further cuts were implemented in the Country Area, but although the Green Line services had suffered the greatest drop in demand in the wake of the strike, no cuts were made to these coach routes. In the November further swingeing cuts were inflicted on Central Area services, with the loss of 371 Mon-Fri buses, 316 on Sats and 504 on Sundays, an overall reduction of some 9%. Coincidental with, and part of, these operational economies was the closure of three bus garages, two elderly – Old Kent Road and Putney Bridge – and one less than eight-years-old, Clapham. And on the delicensing of the individual buses affected by these cuts were six of those stored RTL, which had been licensed for the first time only six months previously; altogether, 320 RTL now went into store.

Single-deckers

In the early autumn, five GS class buses (Guy Special/ECW B26F) were hired to Great Yarmouth Corporation Transport with a view to a sale, but in the event they were returned to London in July 1959, the Norfolk operator preferring the Albion Nimbus/ Willowbrook combination. The 14T12 type (1946 AEC Regal 0662/Weymann) was withdrawn on 25 November, leaving Central Area saloon work in the hands of the RF and TD (Leyland Tiger PS1/Mann Egerton), apart from three Country Area 15T13s (AEC Regal III/Mann Egerton) on route 201. Anticipated for late 1958 had been the delivery of the first production Routemasters, but none was forthcoming save for RM8, exhibited at that year's Commercial Motor Show and destined to be a Chiswick Works experimental vehicle until 1976, and with the large number of RT and RTL buses made surplus with the various service cuts, it was decided that the first three stages of the trolleybus conversion scheme would be with these buses rather than with the Routemaster. **CB**

In preparing this piece, my thanks go to old friend Paul Bateson of Brampton Transit, Canada, for providing 'memory-jogging notes', and acknowledgement is given of the references made to Buses Illustrated *and the* London Bus Magazine.

The Country Area cuts had made inroads into the 'minibus' GS class and LTE was seeking buyers for these barely five-year-old buses. In the autumn of 1958 five were hired to Great Yarmouth Corporation with a view to a sale, which was not forthcoming.

25 November 1958 saw the last day of the type 14T12. These 50 decidedly-provincial AEC Regal I 0662 with 7.7-litre engines, manual transmission and less-than-London-style Weymann bodies, had given stalwart service over many parts of the system. Earlier in 1958 T763 nears the Greenford terminus of the then 211 route.

NORTHERN IN GENERAL

The Northern General group of companies could always be relied on for vehicle variety. Photos from the PHOTOBUS collection

The British Electric Traction company (BET) set up Northern General Transport in 1913 to consolidate its interests in the northeast of England. Over the years it assumed responsibility for other BET bus interests in the area, starting with Gateshead & District in 1914, then Tynemouth & District, Wakefield's Motors, Sunderland District, Tyneside Tramways & Tramroads, and in 1970 Venture Transport.

Separate fleetnames and liveries were retained right up to the formation of the National Bus Company, but as the core of today's Go-Ahead Group, several of the old registered company names survives, even if the fleetnames have been updated. **CB**

The Gateshead & District Tramways Co operated steam trams from 1883 and electric trams from 1901; trams ran into Newcastle from 1923 until 1951. Although trolleybuses had originally been considered to replace the trams, motorbuses were used – Guy Arabs and Leyland Titans. Gateshead & District Omnibus Co No 50 (CCN 150), a Leyland Titan PD2/3 with 56-seat Leyland bodywork, was new in 1951, one of a large batch of Titans bought to complete the tramway replacement.
Gordon Turner/Photobus

Gateshead & District adopted this green/cream livery in 1964, as worn here by No 129 (BCN 529C), a 1965 Leyland Atlantean PDR1/1 with Alexander 75-seat body, one of 10 bought in 1965. It is seen in Gateshead.
Arnold Richardson/Photobus

The splendidly-named Tyneside Tramways & Tramroads Co operated electric trams from 1902 until 1930, although the name only changed to Tyneside Omnibus Co Ltd in 1965. The small bus fleet was exclusively Leyland for many years and No 49 (NNL 49), seen in Wallsend garage in 1969, was one of three Leyland Titan PD3/4 with Metro-Cammell Orion 73-seat bodies bought in 1958.
Arnold Richardson/Photobus

Above: **What became the Tynemouth & District Transport Co started as a tramway company in 1890, first with steam trams and from 1899 with electric trams; the last trams ran in 1931. The largely double-deck bus fleet, Daimlers, Guys and Leylands in the years since World War 2, included a number of early Leyland Atlantean PDR1/1, like No 248 (DFT 248) with a rather ungainly Roe 78-seat body, new in 1960 and seen in Percy Main Garage in 1969.** *Arnold Richardson/Photobus*

Below: **The private company, Wakefield's Motors Ltd, was set up in 1927 and acquired by Northern General two years later. The small Wakefield's fleet shared the livery and Percy Main garage with the larger Tynemouth company, and No 304 (EFT 704F), a 1968 Leyland Leopard PSU3/4R with 47-seat Alexander Y type body, is seen in Percy Main in 1969.** *Arnold Richardson/Photobus*

Above: **Gateshead & District took delivery of 10 early Leyland Atlantean PDR1/1 in 1959 with the early style of Alexander 78-seat body. No 83 (KCN 183) is seen in central Newcastle.**
Gordon Turner/Photobus

Below: **Tyneside No 45 (GTY 175) was one of nine Leyland Titan PD2/12 bought in 1954 with early examples of the Metro-Cammell Orion 58-seat body. It is seen in Newcastle.**
Gordon Turner/Photobus

Above: **Tynemouth & District ran a number of Guy Arab III in the postwar period. No 168 (FT 6568), a 1949 example, carries rare Pickering 56-seat bodywork.**
Gordon Turner/Photobus

Below: **The Wakefield's fleet included a number of coaches, like No 192 (FT 7792), a 39-seat Beadle semi-integral, built around older AEC Regal units.**
Gordon Turner/Photobus

Above: **The Sunderland District Omnibus Co Ltd also had its roots in a tramway operation – its predecessors ran electric trams between 1905 and 1925, until motorbus competition forced closure. Northern General acquired the company in 1931. No 315 (2315 PT), seen at Sunderland Park Lane bus station in 1968, is a 1961 Leyland Tiger Cub PSUC1/1 with BET-style Alexander 45-seat body.**
Arnold Richardson/Photobus

Below: **Sunderland bus station again, and Sunderland District No 303 (603 EUP) displays the distinctive SDO dark blue/white livery to advantage. It is a 1959 Leyland Atlantean PDR1/1 with 78-seat Alexander body. Behind is a Northern Atlantean/Roe.**
Arnold Richardson/Photobus

Above: **The parent Northern General Transport Co Ltd, formed in 1913, built up a substantial empire by expansion and acquisition. Low bridges meant that the Northern fleet always included a large number of maximum-capacity single-deckers. No 1823 (HCN 123) is a 1958 AEC Reliance MU3RV with 45-seat Burlingham body, seen in Sunderland in 1968.**
Arnold Richardson/Photobus

Below: **Probably the most distinctive double-deckers in the Northern fleet were the 50 Leyland-engined AEC/Park Royal forward entrance Routemasters bought in 1964/5. No 2092 (RCN 692) of the 1964 batch is pictured in Sunderland during 1970. London Transport's solitary forward-entrance Routemaster, RMF1254, joined the Northern fleet in 1966.**
Roy Marshall/Photobus

Above: *Guy double-deck and single-deck buses were favoured by Northern General in the postwar years. Two Arab III are seen: No 1427 (CCN 427) of 1952 with Weymann 56-seat body, alongside No 1190 (GUP 790) with locally-built Northern Coachbuilders body.*
Gordon Turner/Photobus

Below: *No 1945 (BCN 823) is a 1950 Arab III with the later, ECW-influenced, style of Northern Coachbuilders 56-seat body, seen here in Chester-le-Street. Note the 'Shop at Binns' advert, characteristic of Northern group buses for many years.*
Gordon Turner/Photobus

Above: **At Marlborough Crescent bus station in Newcastle, Northern No 2262 (FT 9917), a 1957 AEC Reliance MU3RV with 43-seat Willowbrook body.**
Gordon Turner/Photobus

Below: **Northern was an early customer for 36ft-long buses when these were legalised. No 2252 (HCU 52) is one of 10 Leyland Leopards with 53-seat Willowbrook bodies bought in 1962. It is at Newcastle's Marlborough Crescent bus station.**
Gordon Turner/Photobus

Above: **Northern No 2332 (ECN 32E) carried the prototype Marshall Camair body mounted on Leyland Leopard PSU3/3R chassis. It is seen at Chester-le-Street in 1968.**
Arnold Richardson/Photobus

Below: **In the early days of NBC, before the standard liveries kicked in, Northern received batches of two-door ECW-bodied 44-seat Bristol RELL6G. KCN 239J of 1971 is seen at Chester-le-Street in 1972.**
Roy Marshall/Photobus

Above: **The Northern group was an early customer for the Leyland National, and received some of the small number of Nationals delivered in company liveries before the NBC standard schemes took over. UUP 831K, a 1151/2R example new in 1972 is seen on the same occasion as the Bristol RELL, also in Northern maroon/cream. It is also a two-door 44-seater.**
Roy Marshall/Photobus

Below: **Sunderland District also took early Nationals, like No 13K (UUP 13K) in full blue/cream at Sunderland Park Lane bus station in 1972.**
Roy Marshall/Photobus

TALE OF THE CENTURY

With 2000 on the horizon, everybody's looking back at the great achievements of the 20th century. GAVIN BOOTH considers the buses of the century

IF THE END of a decade is excuse enough to look back at the highlights of the previous 10 years, then the end of a century – indeed, the end of a millennium – is a golden opportunity for writers to sit at their word-processors and ruminate on the significant events of the past 2,000 years. As 1999 progresses we will be deluged with articles about The Record of the Century, The Man of the Millennium, The Best Book of All Time.

With buses it's a bit easier. Although the first motorbuses rumbled on to the streets of Britain just before the end of the last century, the first recognisable buses were 20th century inventions, and the past 100 years have seen the bus industry grow – slowly at first, and then with a mid-century gallop – before starting a slow but steady decline that has been partly arrested by the twin '-ations' of the past 20 years, deregulation and privatisation, and, it must be acknowledged, by a growing concern about traffic congestion and a latter-day recognition that the humble bus is a practical and environmentally-friendly beast.

During 1999 in the magazine *Classic Bus* we shall be inviting readers to nominate the Classic Bus of the Century, as a prelude to an event planned for 2000. This article in no way attempts to influence readers – the very thought! – but draws together some loose strands about just what criteria might be used to make such a judgement.

Amazingly significant

There have been some amazingly significant buses built over the past century. Some were staggeringly innovative, though perhaps they didn't set the heather on fire in sales terms; others have been real lemons, immortalised in Alan Millar's regular Classic Blunderbus column in the magazine. And many, many more have been straightforward, unexciting workhorses that helped to make money for their owners and their manufacturers. This is certainly an over-simplification, but it helps to concentrate the mind.

Then there's the London Factor.

There are readers of *Classic Bus* who have an unwavering loyalty towards London Transport, its policies and its buses. Who will hear no ill of anything that LT did, and defend it to the last.

Too 'ordinary' to be one of the 20th century's classic buses? The AEC Reliance, a popular and hard-working chassis, with Plaxton Panorama coach body on the Esplanade of Edinburgh Castle in 1967. NRD 155D was owned by World Wide Coaches.
All photos by Gavin Booth except where otherwise credited

There are others, usually living outside London, who are cynical about LT and wonder just what all the fuss is all about.

And there are those, probably the majority, who respect the lead that LT gave to the bus industry in so many areas, not least bus design, but recognise that equally important things were happening in 'the provinces' and point to some well-publicised LT disasters as proof that not everything was quite as rosy as it was painted.

That said, as for much of this century London General/London Transport were by far the biggest bus operators in Britain, their influence was undoubtedly significant, though sheer numbers of buses don't always equate with innovation, reliability or quality.

So it is inevitable that there are London models that will feature in our eventual millennium hall of fame, but equally inevitable that some popular London classes won't.

Earliest days

Look back at the earliest days of the motorbus, when the new petrol engine technology was being applied to vehicles that would otherwise be horse-drawn. Many manufacturers dabbled in motorbus and motor lorry manufacture, but few enjoyed real success and even fewer survived.

London General approached the motorbus very cautiously, and when it eventually took the plunge and embarked on production of double-deck buses for its own use, the design was 'cribbed shamelessly', to quote General's chief engineer, Frank Searle, to produce the X type in 1909. Dubbed the 'Daimler-Wolseley-Straker' by some, alluding to its ancestry in existing London types, experience with the X type led to the legendary B type in 1910, and this went into mass production; some 2,700 were in service at the outbreak of World War 1, and the last B type double-deckers survived in London until 1926.

If the B type is the bus most people instinctively think of as representative of the pre-1914 years, this undervalues the Milnes-Daimler, the 'Daimler' in the mixed parentage of the London X type. Tramcar builders, G. F. Milnes & Co, became agents for the German Daimler company in 1902 and developed the Milnes-Daimler, first in single-deck form, and from

Above left: *The London General B type was one of the first significant motorbus types. B340 from the London Transport Collection is seen in its one-time home at Clapham.*

Left: *Most CB readers will really only know the Leyland Titan TD1 through the handful of preserved examples. Two, ex-Bolton WH 1553 and ex-Southern National DR 4902, are seen together on Brighton seafront at the end of the 1970 HCVC Brighton Run.*

Above: *The uncompromising lines of preserved Swindon Corporation utility Guy Arab DHR 192, a 1943 example with Weymann bodywork.*

Below: *The AN68 series Leyland Atlantean was regarded as a vast improvement on the earlier PDR versions. National Bus Company took Atlanteans in the 1970s to speed vehicle deliveries, AN68/1R models with Park Royal 71-seat bodies. London Country Nos AN122/3 are seen at Chessington Zoo on private hire duties when new in 1974.*

Above: **While many operators liked the Bristol VRT, others were less happy. Tayside Regional Council bought 25 VRTLL in 1977 with Alexander 83-seat bodies, but had disposed of them within a few years. Two are seen in Dundee High Street.**

Below: **Designed as Leyland's all-purpose double-decker, the integral TN15 Titan only really found favour in London. The biggest customer outside London was Greater Manchester PTE with just 15; No 4011 of 1980 is seen at Stockport when new.**

1904 as a double-decker. It was the first really successful motorbus, but its success was cut short by the decision of its major customer, the London Motor Omnibus Co – trading as Vanguard – to turn to building its own chassis. And World War 1 was the final straw for companies relying on supplies from Germany.

If the pre-WW1 candidates for the Classic Bus of the Century are probably few and far between, after the war the situation became much more complex. Although there were still many manufacturers competing for orders in the 1920s and 1930s, periods of dramatic growth for the relatively young bus industry, it could be argued that few produced models that could be considered classics.

Gradually a few major players emerged to dominate the industry, and these manufacturers, with the resources to commit to research and development, tended to produce the models that might be considered as memorable. But not always.

Gilford, that fascinating chassis builder which blossomed for about a decade in the 1920s and 1930s, built a remarkable lowfloor, lowheight front-wheel drive double-decker in 1931. Northern General, operating intensive services in northeast England, developed the advanced side-engined SE4 and SE6 single-deck models for its own use in the 1930s.

Still-familiar names

And even still-familiar names that were active between the wars were really not in the major league at this time. But that didn't mean that they were unadventurous. Guy and Maudslay, for example, developed the first low-frame chassis that were more suitable for bus and coach use than previous lorry-based types, and Dennis pioneered the use of four-wheel brakes.

Bristol and Daimler were late developers. Both companies had been building buses since the early part of the century, but it took the introduction of Gardner diesel-engined chassis in the mid-1930s to propel them into the big league, where they would stay for the next 40 years.

But AEC and Leyland were the undoubted leaders among the builders of heavyweight chassis, and in the 1930s Bedford quickly established itself as the leading builder of lighter chassis.

AEC built vast quantities of its Regal and Regent chassis from 1929 until war interrupted production. The success and popularity of these types would undoubtedly guarantee them a place in the 20th century hall of fame, but with what bodywork? London fans would doubtless nominate the ST or, more likely, STL type Regents with classic Chiswick-built LPTB bodies, but what about a nice municipal Regent, maybe for Brighton or Leeds, or for a company fleet like Western Welsh.

AEC worked closely with London General and then London Transport on the side-engined Q type; is this a Classic Bus of the Century, or just a short-lived curio that never quite succeeded?

Mind you, that description couldn't be laid at the door of another AEC/LT partnership, the Regent RT, which in 1939 redefined double-deckers at a stroke, and set a pattern for the next 15 years until its successor was ready.

The secret of the Bristol Lodekka's success was its low-slung chassis allowing normal seating on both decks within the 'lowbridge' overall height. This is the interior of the 1949 prototype.
BTCC

Leyland had earlier redefined double-deckers with its Titan TD1 model in 1927, representing an amazing advance on anything that had been seen before. A fairly certain CBotC candidate, perhaps – but how do you treat the mould-breaking underfloor-engined TF and rear-engined CR types built for London Transport? Interesting, certainly, and like the AEC Q they were models that gave manufacturers and operators good first-hand experience of alternative engine positions; had World War 2 not intervened, we would surely have seen underfloor- and rear-engined chassis earlier than we did.

Was the utility Guy Arab a CBotC? Many would argue that this rugged chassis did much to keep Britain moving during the war. It was not innovative in any way, but it was pretty indestructible and reliable, which was exactly what was wanted.

Popularity

If sheer popularity counts towards the CBotC title, then the Bedford OB must be a contender. This simple chassis, typically married to a Duple Vista coach body, seemed to be ubiquitous in the early postwar years, and helped operators of all sizes to get back into the coach touring business after the war.

We haven't mentioned Midland Red, whose SOS chassis tended to be quirky and hardly ground-breaking. Until the war years, at least, when with Donald Sinclair at the helm, BMMO investigated rear-engined single-deckers, and then, virtually as soon as

The main rival to the Leyland Titan was the MCW Metrobus, which won London orders but won favour with other major customers. Strathclyde PTE No MB34, a MkII example, is seen when new in 1983.

the war had ended, swung into production with its underfloor-engined S6 type, when the commercial manufacturers were churning out traditional chassis to satisfy the export drive and the insatiable appetite for new buses.

Bristol, too, seemed to be resting on its reputation for safe and unspectacular chassis, until in 1949 it unveiled the lowheight Lodekka model, probably a CBotC. Then it went back to solid, unexciting, reliable models until the RE came along in 1962.

The RE challenged the accepted notion of the single-deck bus. Since the early 1950s horizontal underfloor engines had been the norm, but the essentially high floors meant that they were not ideal for intensive urban work. Rear engines mounted under the floor at the rear allowed the area ahead of the rear axle to be at a much lower level, and though models like the AEC Swift and Leyland Panther enjoyed brief success in some of the larger fleets, they proved to be less durable than the RE. But while the RE was the first, and probably the best, of the 1960s rear-engined buses, it had been Leyland that introduced the layout on a widespread scale.

The rear-engined Leyland Atlantean went into production in 1958 and although it undoubtedly broke the double-deck mould, it wasn't a CBotC from the start. Early Atlanteans were notoriously troublesome,

but the later AN68 series got it right, as did the rival Fleetline from Daimler. So does the Atlantean make the CBotC list because it was innovative, because of the sheer numbers built, or because it was ultimately a successful bus?

The Atlantean went into production at the same time as the Routemaster, probably the ultimate development of the traditional British front-engined/rear-entrance double-decker. Still serving London 40 years on, the RM will undoubtedly be a contender for the CBotC title for many readers. But where does that place models like the AEC Regent, Daimler CVD/CVG or Leyland Titan PD? All were steady sellers in the 20 years after the war, and gained a reputation for being dependable buses. Not earth-shatteringly innovative, perhaps, but they moved millions of passengers without fuss.

Then there were the models produced with London orders in mind, like the Leyland Titan TN15 or the MCW Metrobus. Both sold well into London, and the Metrobus enjoyed wider popularity. But CBotC?

Sheer numbers

On the basis of sheer numbers, many of the underfloor-engined single-deckers of the 1950s and 1960s would justify places in the list. But best-selling types like the AEC Reliance, Bristol LS/MW or Leyland Leopard were hardly ground-breaking designs; they were really just competent buses that sold in substantial quantities.

The Leyland National had the single-deck citybus market virtually to itself during much of the 1970s, and pioneered mass production techniques that were revolutionary at the time, but which have never been seen again in the UK. The lack of any real competition meant that the National, never, in all honesty, the most popular model, sold in impressive quantities, and can hardly be ignored when considering the CBotC.

Recently – and normally strictly outwith CB's remit – some notable models have emerged which must surely be CBotC contenders. Take the Volvo B10M, a straightforward underfloor-engined chassis which has sold in impressive quantities in the UK, in bus and coach form, and throughout the world. But in UK terms is the B10M any more deserving of a CBotC place than its Leopard or Reliance predecessors?

And there's the Olympian, successor to the Atlantean, Fleetline and Bristol VRT. Like the B10M it has been in production for nearly 20 years, and has been double-deck market leader for most of that time. It first appeared in 1980 as a Bristol designed and built underframe before production moved to Leyland and Workington and it was subsequently taken over by Volvo, and built at Irvine. An undoubtedly competent and successful bus, but a CBotC?

Probably the most obvious CBotC contender among recent models is the Dennis Dart, the rear-engined midibus chassis that outsells every other single-deck bus. This meets all the criteria – it was innovative, it has sold well, and it has proved successful.

Your chance

Classic Bus magazine readers will have the chance to make their views known during 1999 when they are invited to nominate contenders for the Classic Bus of the Century title. Their nominations will reflect their age, where they live, their prejudices – which is the way it should be. There are some obvious contenders for the title, but there will undoubtedly be others that attract a significant vote.

The results of the poll will be announced in CB later in the year and it is hoped to mount a gathering of as many of the winning types as possible during the course of 2000. This article should set you thinking. Keep watching the magazine for details of how you can register your vote to help us establish the Classic Bus of the Century. **CB**

Above: *For many the ultimate in double-deckers is the Routemaster. RM664, the experimental unpainted version, on the Embankment on an Omnibus Society tour.*

Left: *The Daimler Fleetline took the rear-engined double-deck concept a step beyond Leyland's earlier Atlantean with a more reliable chassis that offered true lowheight bodies. These three North Western Fleetlines are awaiting completion at the Alexander coachworks at Falkirk in 1964.*

'PETROL' BUSES REIGN SUPREME

THOMAS W. W. KNOWLES worked at Derby Corporation when its last trolleybuses were replaced by 'petrol' buses

Derby disasters included loss of power to the overhead. This power cut in 1966 caused a line up of depot- and Harvey Road-bound trolleybuses as they hit the dead section. The first two trolleybuses are Willowbrook-bodied Sunbeam F4s of 1952/3.

All black-and-white photos by T. W. W. Knowles

IT ALWAYS struck me as odd that the longer-serving members of Derby Corporation Omnibus Department's staff distinguished between the trolleybuses and motorbuses by referring to the latter as 'petrol' buses – the more up-to-date called them 'oilers'!

I had lived in Derby for over three years, working for Trent, before I moved to the Corporation as a traffic assistant, and it was evident that the organisation was not the most up-to-date in the land, and the aforementioned was perhaps indicative of the way DCOD thought about and did things. When I started work there in October 1966 the most recent senior outside appointment was the rolling stock superintendent who had joined the organisation at the end of the war in 1945!

Above: *Typical of the relaxed utility Park Royal-bodied Sunbeam Ws is No 185 seen at Midland Station.*
J. Copland/Photobus

Below: *Contrasting the Brush and Willowbrook bodies on Derby Sunbeam F4s. No 214 of 1949 with Brush body and No 234 of 1953 with Willowbrook body. Both buses were withdrawn in 1967.*
J. Copland/Photobus

A Market Place panorama with Sunbeam F4/Willowbrook No 220 and the rear of No 242, a 1960 Sunbeam F4A/Roe.
Roy Marshall/Photobus

So what did I find? Well, the motorbus fleet was decidedly ancient but in somewhat better condition than the trolleybus fleet. You see, at Trent there were a number of enthusiasts of my age group. and we used to ride on Corporation buses and trolleys for the fun and laughs we used to get. In those days. buses were subjected to Certificates of Fitness which ensured that every few years (the interval generally reducing as the bus got older) buses had to be presented to the ministry certifying officer in sound condition whilst in the in-between years. a less taxing inspection was carried out by the vehicle inspector. Even so, this did not stop the amusement caused to us when travelling on the Brush-bodied buses where the floor upstairs moved in a different direction from the upper part of the body! No doubt this was in part a result of what I gather had been the Brush construction method of building the upper and lower decks separately and bolting together during build. Mind you, Brush, who came from Loughborough only 20 miles away, by this time had ceased building buses, although Derby still ran examples on Daimler Crossley and Foden motorbuses. as well as Sunbeam trolleybuses.

Riding on the motorbuses was nothing compared with the trolleybuses. A favourite seat on which to travel on the latter was the side seat inside the rear entrance over the wheelarch – or what was left of it, as one looked down and saw the road speeding past underneath where we sat! Cleaning methods were something else!

Decision to abandon

By the time I moved to DCOD, the decision to abandon the trolleybus system had been made, and one of my tasks was to schedule the duties and bus workings as each stage progressed. Although they had been a familiar sight whilst I was at Trent, the two utility Sunbeam Ws with Weymann bodywork had been withdrawn in 1965 whilst the relaxed utility Sunbeam Ws had finally been eliminated early in 1966 when 20 years old; these had been bodied by Park Royal and seemed sounder than their younger Brush bodied counterparts.

The remainder of the trolleybus fleet comprised three batches. Withdrawals had already commenced on the 30 Brush-bodied Sunbeam F4s which had been new in 1945/9 although a couple – Nos 207/15 (ARC 507/15) – survived to the last stage. There were 20 further Sunbeam F4s which came in 1952/3, the bodies of which were ordered from Brush but were built by neighbouring Willowbrook after it acquired the Brush order book. One of these, No 216 (DRC 216), was exhibited at the 1952 Commercial Motor Show and the whole batch survived into 1967 when some were withdrawn at the penultimate conversion. The third batch were actually rather splendid and always seemed to be in better condition than other vehicles in the fleet, even allowing for their age. Although there were only eight trolleybuses in the

Above: *The first relaxed utility trolleybus was withdrawn in 1963 along with some postwar Brush-bodied Sunbeam F4s. Their replacements were Roe-bodied Daimler CVG6s, one of the batch of which was No 146 seen here in 1969 on a former trolleybus route to Upperdale Road.*

Below: *The Omnibus Society visited Derby on the last Sunday of operation, 3 September 1967, and amongst other activities was this wrong-running performed by show bus No 216 (1952 Earls Court Commercial Motor Show) in Ascot Drive, outside the depot.*

Two of the four ex-Halifax Daimler CVG6s with MCW bodies bought to enable the final conversion stage to be completed are seen behind Ascot Drive Depot in 1969.

batch new ground was broken by them having Roe teak-framed bodies fitted to their Sunbeam F4A chassis. Built in 1960, so successful were these vehicles that Roe became Derby's standard body supplier for many years on both Daimler CVG6 and Daimler Fleetline chassis. Because they had higher seating capacities – 65 as against 56 or 60 – these trolleybuses were usually to be found on the busy Shelton Lock route. No 236 (SCH 936) was unusual in having an automatic accelerator which was removed upon withdrawal and sold with another vehicle from the batch (No 237) for preservation.

At its maximum, the Derby trolleybus system comprised 27.91 miles of overhead. but by the time of my arrival, this had been reduced to 21.01 miles. The first conversion in which I was involved took place in November 1966. almost a year since the previous conversion, which saw the official withdrawal of Sinfin Lane trolleybuses. This was typical of DCOD's conversions in that although regular trolleybus services were withdrawn from both Uttoxeter Road and Normanton Road, the wiring remained in place for 'specials', ie works and school journeys. This stage saw the withdrawal of a number of Brush-bodied Sunbeam F4s, most of which found their way to Autospares of Bingley (Yorkshire) where some survived for several years in its quarry.

Caution prevails

Every time a conversion took place, economies were made with the schedules such that trolleybuses were not replaced on a one-for-one basis. With the November 1966 conversion, 15 new buses arrived. All were Roe-bodied Daimlers but in true Derby style, caution prevailed and whereas 10 were Fleetlines

(KRC 175-84D) of a similar style to three delivered in January 1966 for evaluation, the remaining five (155-9) were what turned out to be the last Daimler CVG6s delivered to Derby – the end of a run of 52 such buses the first of which came in 1961.

This period was significant for its staff shortages. If Rolls-Royce was on full-time working, it seemed that most other employers in the town struggled for staff. In fact there was a shortage of trolleybus and motorbus drivers as well as conductors so although the end of the trolleybus system was in sight, training of drivers continued. It always amused me to see a trolleybus in service with the driver under tuition and showing 'L' plates; such were the regulations. On certain routes where the wiring had not been pulled down, motorbus drivers who held trolleybus licences drove trolleybuses on officially withdrawn routes. You can imagine the problems this caused with arranging reliefs! Anyhow trolleybus driver training continued until early February 1967. a few days before the penultimate conversion took place.

This stage was relatively small in vehicle working terms. but achieved the trolleybus withdrawal of the Kedleston Road route which was operationally severed from London Road. together with the conversion of special workings on Uttoxeter Road and Normanton Road. However, the odd special still used Uttoxeter Road after this date when there was a shortage of

Below: *Carrying bodywork similar to contemporary Derby trolleybuses is No 75, a Brush-bodied Daimler CVD6 of 1949.*
Arnold Richardson/
Photobus

Apart from the four secondhand buses from Halifax, the batch of new buses purchased for the final conversion included Roe-bodied Daimler Fleetline NCH 192E.

motorbus drivers or vehicles. The last recorded special ran in May 1967 and the wiring was removed by the end of July. Kedleston Road was never used again and was dismantled immediately whilst the Normanton Road wiring remained intact until the end – being used by extras on the last day, accompanied by much sparking on the early journeys! This stage was achieved without any new motorbuses being introduced into the fleet: trolleybus casualties included the first of the DRC batch of Sunbeams new in 1952/3.

Final conversion

As the months went past, so the due date for the final conversion drew near; it was to be 9 September 1967. If major repairs were needed on any surviving trolleybus the vehicle was taken out of service whilst the overhead wiring seemed to become slacker and slacker. Derby was noted amongst visiting enthusiasts for the ample opportunities to observe dewirements and whereas every effort was made to provide a reliable service this was extremely difficult with the staff shortages. The staff we had were not all happy either; as we approached conversion day reluctant ex-trolleybus drivers were finding it hard to learn to drive

a bus – something they had never chosen to do anyhow – whilst the tightening of schedules was less than popular. In fact I remember that I worked through the night to complete the final rosters since the unions had rejected them yet again. It was interesting that although the union officials were anti-establishment, when the branch secretary realised the consequences of their action so far as I was concerned, a hot flask appeared at some unearthly hour to help sustain me!

As the last day approached, it had become evident that the 15 new buses on order were not quite enough to complete the conversion. The last set of trolleybus schedules had a morning peak output of 21 and it had been hoped to save enough workings through the integration of the schedules to complete the exercise with the Fleetlines that were due and turned out to be NCH 190-204E. What was to be done?

In 1971, Brush-bodied ARC 505 still lay at Autospares premises just outside Bingley, Yorkshire.

Talk of retaining the Shelton Lock service took place, but this gave too many trolley vehicles left in service; works and school specials could be retained but this meant the maintenance of too much of the overhead for little use as well as the retention of the overhead gangs, although they would also be dismantling the redundant wiring. In the end an unusual solution for those days was found, and this was to purchase four buses from Halifax Corporation Transport. These buses were Daimler CVG6s with MCW bodies (DCP 549-52) and were given fleet numbers 49-52 by Derby. Thus 19 motorbuses replaced 26 trolleybuses.

Last day

As the last day approached, it was clear to the management at DCOD that considerable interest had been generated amongst the enthusiast fraternity and it was decided to put on special services on the last day to cover wiring that was still in place. A three-bus cycle was devised which took six hours to complete(!) and this ran from mid-morning to about 22.00hrs. After that the workings were scheduled to carry out duplication on last buses on selected routes. Sadness and celebration were the order of the day; Ron Johnson signed his bus off as 'very sad' whilst Mohan Singh, for one, bedecked his trolleybus with balloons.

The fun came with the race to make sure who was the last bus in depot. In the event, a very smart B. K. Fletcher arrived with a very full No 236 sometime after midnight to take the honours amidst a huge cheer from several hundred onlookers. He was not noted for running late, but he did on this occasion!

The next day was a Sunday and was very flat. There were still enthusiasts, and I regret to say souvenir hunters at Ascot Drive depot but out on the road the 'petrol' buses had taken over and now reigned supreme. One good thing from the point of view of the bus. as opposed to the trolleybus, enthusiast was that the life of the early postwar Daimler CVD6s – some now 20 years old – Crossleys and Fodens was extended and a few of these Daimlers and some Crossleys which had manual gearboxes and thus were used for driver training, survived into 1970. **CB**

ISLE OF MAN BUSES AND COACHES
ON OLD PICTURE POSTCARDS

PETER AND JUDY DEEGAN dip into their postcard collection to provide a glimpse of halcyon days on the Isle of Man

An unusual marque was purchased by McMillan's 'The Huntsman Motors' in May 1929: MN 3808 is a Detroit-built Denby, almost certainly designed as a small lorry (a larger chassis for motor coaches was introduced in 1927). This Rushen Abbey view appears to have been taken shortly after purchase, and the coachbuilder's transfer tells us that it was constructed by Massey Bros of Wigan. Sixteen passengers are on board the 15-seat coach: presumably the small child travelled on a relative's knee! The driver may be seen sitting in the second seat from the right-hand side, a position dictated by the location of the steering wheel (adding weight to the suggestion that the chassis was not designed to carry four people on the front seat). It must be assumed that hand signals were not to be expected by traffic following behind.

All photos from Peter Deegan collection

THE STUDY of the early days of road passenger travel is often spoiled by the absence of sufficient suitable photographic sources, but one possible line of investigation that may help to redress the balance is to search for suitable material at the many antique and postcard fairs held at regular intervals across the United Kingdom.

In a collection that now numbers several thousand cards, we have found that street scenes have provided us with many examples of topographical cards depicting various modes of transport 'in action'. Other sources provide examples of posed shots, in the form of advertising cards illustrating the product of bodybuilders and or chassis makers, or even used by operators to illustrate the latest marque of coach available for hire by groups.

The heyday of the charabanc was a prolific period for the photographer, as the open vehicles were most suitable for a posed group shot that could yield useful bulk sales on the return of the outing. Some locations became the regular 'haunt' of photographers: the cliffs

at Bournemouth, Torre station (between Torquay and Paignton), the Railway Wall at Southport, and the Promenade at Rhyl (White Rose kept the sales in-house by employing its own photographer); even the Llanberis Pass had its resident cameraman ready to provide a souvenir of an exhilarating drive through the mountains. The subsequent development of the all-weather coach reduced the market significantly, although enterprising cameramen cajoled tourists into posing in front of the coach (spoiling the effect from a purely historical viewpoint) or even persuading the passengers to stand on their seats so that a head-and-shoulders view through the rolled-back roof might be had.

In the collection in this feature, we hope to recall that the Isle of Man has a fascinating road transport history, not least due to the longevity of its vehicles as a result of the short tourist season, and the limited road mileage within the shores of this small Kingdom. The popular Manx photo-spots were located at Rushen Abbey in the southern part of the island, and at Sulby Glen in the north: both were popular tea-stops on the tours. **CB**

Standing only a few yards from Douglas Harbour, the Victoria Clock Tower stood between the town centre terminus of the now defunct Douglas Cable Tramway (approaching from the left along Victoria Street) and the still-extant horse tramway. In this mid-1920s view it is surprising that neither form of transport is in sight, although a sign on the Tower advises that the 'last cars leave at ll.20pm'. Heading towards the harbour is one of Douglas Corporation's normal-control Tilling-Stevens petrol electric omnibuses, still running on solid tyres. Douglas purchased eight of these machines between 1914 and 1923, and all survived until 1934. The card, postmarked 1927, does not bear a maker's mark, but the view was still in the postcard racks 10 years later!

Farther round Douglas Bay stands the Villa Marina entertainment complex, running from near to the Sefton Hotel to the Broadway junction (where the cable tramcars reached the front again after their semi-circular journey through Upper Douglas). This Valentine card, taken from the roof of the colonnade in 1934, shows no fewer than eight touring coaches on the stand, with a ninth heading towards the harbour. Even at this late date a charabanc is visible, along with the all-weather and saloon coaches: on a warm summers day there was a high regard for tours by the open machines. Five horse-trams (including one double-decker) can be seen heading for Derby Castle, perhaps indicating that the view was taken at the onset of the morning 'peak' with holidaymakers expected to be making their way to the front to be cajoled into a motor tour, or to board the horse trams to reach the electric cars to Laxey and Ramsey. Beneath the balustrade of the Villa Marina may be seen the roofs of two Isle of Man Road Services omnibuses.

From the north end of Douglas the coast road snakes on to Onchan Head to pass the Imperial Hotel and reach Port Jack, where a row of shops beckons souvenir-hunters. In this Lilywhite view Douglas Corporation's AEC Regent double-deck bus No 42 (MN 8691) with Northern Counties body appears to be about to overtake the solitary car, while a Manx Electric car and trailer climb past the

shops en route for Laxey. The bus, new in 1933, survived in the Douglas fleet until 1957 although this early postwar view could just have easily been shot in the prewar period, the Bedford OB coach parked on the pavement in front of Stead House gives the only clue as to the period.

The adage that 'the camera cannot lie' is disproved by this Manx Electric Railway Official Card (produced by Valentines), depicting three of the Railway's Argus lorry/charas linking the railway with Sulby Glen from Bungalow station of the Snaefell Mountain Railway (a Snaefell car is seen in the middle background). The card bears Valentine's number 21916, which should indicate a view taken in 1894, but of course the Mountain Railway was not constructed until 1895, and the Bungalow Hotel was built in the following year! Probably the original version carried an artist's impression and the card number of this 'dedicated' view was crystallised by the manufacturer when the card was 'updated'. Even this was not the extent of the deceit, for the electric car is seen in its post-1900 form and the distant view of the stone-built Summit Hotel is drawn in — the original building was constructed of wood. An examination of the charas shows the two on the right have been superimposed on the picture, as they are not 'in scale'; they are seen to be MN 67 and MN 68 and these were the two Argus machines. The third machine must also be one of these two vehicles, for the Railway only owned two Argus and it seems that the third was superimposed around 1914 when a De Dion joined the fleet. 'Doctoring' the picture to meet the requirements of the railway was presumably simpler than despatching a photographer from Dundee to take a new negative!

Two coaches that had unusually short lives in service were the Bedford WLBs purchased by the Manx Electric Railway in April and May 1939 to operate the link between the Snaefell Mountain cars at Bungalow station and Sulby Glen. The second of these, MN 8874, is seen in this RA Series card in its 1939 season at the Tholt-y-Will Hotel at Sulby Glen; after a long period laid up during the war, little use was made of the coaches in postwar days until sale at the beginning of the 1953 season. MN 8874 saw

further service (as a goods van) for four years before final withdrawal. It had originally been owned by Corkhill of Onchan, and was new in 1933.

The early history of the omnibus in the Isle of Man reveals a period of competition in which several companies sought to obtain supremacy. In due time takeovers and amalgamations brought almost all the routes into the control of the Isle of Man Railway Company, and the operations were centralised on the Isle of Man Road Services Ltd. Manxland Bus Services Ltd was a company in the British Automobile Traction Co Ltd group, controlled by Cumberland Motor Services Ltd, from which company many of the buses were transferred. A total of 13 Associated Daimler Company (ADC) vehicles was placed on the island in two batches (the

second 'wave' of eight buses being allocated to the fleet of Manx Motors Ltd), and both batches were transferred to the railway company in 1929, and to the Road Services the following year. Withdrawal took place between 1937 and 1950. This unmarked card shows one of the ADC buses running on Crossack Road, Ballasalla, on the route thence to Peel: the small-diameter front tyres suggest that the view is taken at an early date.

W. C. Shimmin's 'Silver Star Motors' operated this 19-seat Vulcan charabanc for 13 years from May 1921; in this view at Rushen Abbey in the latter half of the 1920s it has acquired pneumatic tyres. A photograph also exists of the same machine with pneumatic front tyres, but retaining the solids at the rear, reflecting one of the ways in which the coaches were 'upgraded' over a period of time. Note the stag's head casting on the radiator cap; this had not been fitted in the earlier photograph. The arm-band seen on the driver's sleeve is that issued to denote that he is licensed by the Douglas Corporation.

The small Fiat was a popular chassis in the 1920s and this example at Rushen Abbey (MN 1736) was purchased by Duggan of Douglas in December 1921, and remained in service until July 1933. Although it was registered as a 14-seater this Round The Island Tour in August 1926 is carrying 16 passengers, and it would seem that the two middle rows each contain five passengers crushed into the four seats: perhaps fortunately the 10 young ladies do not appear to be overweight! The proprietor was probably mindful of the fact that peak traffic was available only for some 11 or 12 weeks of the year, and was persuaded to risk the possible wrath of the Douglas Hackney Carriage Inspector on this account.

I WAS THERE

Transport journalist, JOHN ALDRIDGE, recalls an experiment that didn't work out

An elderly lady gives a glance to Silent Rider as it makes a demonstration run along the Cromwell Road . . . or perhaps she is looking at the British Airways poster.
John Aldridge collection

IT IS STRANGE how some of the threads that form part of one's knowledge (or even just views) can not only circulate in one's mind for many years, but can still be as true today as originally. A recent example for me was on an, unexpected, ride on an lpg-powered bus. It was unexpected in that I just happened to be in the right place at the right time and was able to make an unplanned trip.

Then, just as 25 years' ago, one of the minor snags with most alternative power sources showed itself again. It is that quietening a major component (such as the engine) on a bus does not usually provide an equivalent overall quietness. Gearbox and or axle whine, suspension and other noises then all come into greater prominence.

So it was back in 1974 when the South East Lancashire and North East Cheshire Passenger Transport Executive and Chloride (or perhaps Chloride and Selnec) officially unveiled Silent Rider. Quieter it was but (internally at least) silent it wasn't. The bus was battery-powered, and even then (as now) we were waiting for an 'imminent' break-through in battery technology by the Americans.

But that is taking an unfair view of the project. In the early 1970s a recent fuel crisis and current growing problems with the supply of oil, plus rising prices and fears that the supply might sooner or later run out, were making some operators think seriously about alternative fuels. The Teesside municipal undertaking was already experimenting with a Daimler Fleetline with lpg-fuelled Rolls-Royce engine, for example. All this – of course – was before North Sea oil was discovered. Selnec, then Britain's second-largest operator, was doing what a large, forward-thinking, undertaking should: to try and be at least half prepared for a future oil crisis. Its involvement in research with battery-electrics was not limited to one supplier: shortly it would be involved with another, with another bus, this time a midi.

The official unveiling and press do for the Silent Rider was in March 1974, in London rather than

Manchester, which shows the importance of the project to the participants. The hope of gaining national press publicity as well as coverage in the technical press was one reason for the choice of location. The 'do' was at the Penta Hotel on London's Cromwell Road, not exactly a central London hotel, but chosen because it had parking space for a large vehicle plus some local roads that would not be too congested for a few demonstration runs to be made. No doubt the other reason was that the location was within easy reach for people from the Department of the Environment and the Department of Trade and Industry, and there were hopes of getting some DTI funding for a future fleet of these vehicles.

The bus had been completed the previous year, and had then undergone trials at the Transport & Road Research Laboratory at Crowthorne, Berks. It had been certified as a psv in the January and, we were told, would be going into service next month – April, that was. In fact another year was to elapse before it went into fare-paying service.

It was based on a Seddon RU rear-engined chassis, suitably strengthened and with uprated suspension: all very necessary given the unladen weight of 12tons 17cwt 2qr (13,081kg). At 10m long, with two doors and 43 seats it was more-or-less a full-sized bus, whereas the slightly later Seddon-Lucas was only a 19-seater, as were the Department of Trade and Industry's Crompton Electricars demonstrators based on Leyland truck chassis, one of which was borrowed by Selnec for two spells in 1974.

Chloride's Silent Rider was a well-researched and developed project. It could travel at up to 40mph, had

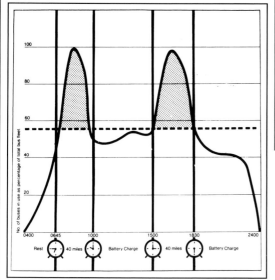

Left: Chloride provided this impressive graph to show the potential for battery-electric buses on peak-hour only work. The grey areas showed the buses could operate with a range of 40 miles before being recharged between peaks.

Below: A gaggle of journalists and photographers look at Silent Rider outside London's Penta Hotel.
John Aldridge collection

Silent Rider is seen in its slightly later, short, life on the Reddish service. It carries Greater Manchester Transport lettering and insignia, but the Selnec name still remains on the fascia of the building behind.
John Aldridge collection

a range of 40 miles, and had regenerative braking which returned some of the energy partially to recharge the battery. It had Sevcon thyristor control (then quite new) to give stepless or smooth acceleration and – inevitably – a separately-powered Webasto heater to provide heating.

Angus Monro, Selnec's director of planning, and his team had looked at other alternatives in the event of future energy shortages, but ultimately ruled out the trolleybus for two reasons. The main one was the cost of the overhead and provision of electrical supplies to it, which would have more than equalled the savings in maintenance costs of a trolleybus compared to a bus. Secondly trolleybuses would have been using the most current at peak times when it was most expensive.

Electric buses, however, would be able to recharge their batteries at off-peak times and were a more suitable solution. Selnec had identified 660 out of its 2,500 buses that worked only at peak times. Even after allowing for the limitations of battery-electrics, it reckoned that rather under 25 per cent of its fleet could be of this type. Interestingly, when Chloride itself studied Selnec's operations at its Hyde Road garage, it concluded that up to 40 per cent of duties could be covered by battery-electrics.

Apparently it was Chloride that approached Selnec with the idea of developing the Silent Rider, and Selnec saw an opportunity to develop a state-of-the-art bus with two particular objectives in mind. These were to quantify the operational advantages of a battery-electric, and to develop control gear and traction equipment which could go into production when the

major breakthrough in electric storage (that is, battery design) occurred, probably 'in the 1980s'. Selnec would then be able to contemplate an immediate production programme.

It was also hoped to get some Government assistance, since a production run of 20 Silent Riders was costed at £75,000 each, against £16,500 for a Leyland Atlantean. Incidentally, the prototype Silent Rider was said to have cost £100,000, a figure I would have thought on the low side, bearing in mind all the research and development costs.

In the end, of course, there never was another energy crisis, and there never were any more Silent Riders either. The one bus led a strange, unhappy life. Selnec and its successor Greater Manchester Transport used the bus at Reddish in the main. But in 445 consecutive days in 1975-76 it was in service there for just 84 days, away on demonstration work for another 80 days, and not available for service for 281 days. Then in 1977 it went to America and was exhibited at the 1st International Electric Vehicle Exposition in Chicago. After the exhibition closed it returned to Manchester, but never ran in service again.

The Silent Rider survives as an exhibit in the Manchester Museum of Transport, along with the battery Seddon Midi. **CB**

BUSES OF ADVERSITY
or
USAGE AND ABUSAGE

ROBERT E. JOWITT dwells in not unsentimental vein – and with the usual diversions – on the adverse fates which befell many classic buses after their withdrawal from public life

GENTLEMENS TOILET

WAY OUT
ENTRANCE OTHER SIDE

BOROUGH OF EPSOM AND EWELL

In the borough engineer's yard (or some such charming spot) in Epsom and/or Ewell in the early 1960s, an ex-Huddersfield Karrier trolleybus waits patiently to be towed up to the Downs on Derby Day to serve a useful – nay vital – function.
All photos by Robert E. Jowitt

I F, IN THE early 1960s, you happened to be at Epsom on Derby Day and, to borrow a polite phrase in vogue at the time, you received a call from nature, or, using a phrase popular with earlier generations, you were taken short, the place to answer the call was in a trolleybus. This was if you happened to be on the wrong side, the plebeian side, of the racecourse; better facilities doubtless existed on the grandstand and royal box side. *Hoi polloi* were provided by the Borough of Epsom & Ewell with a fleet of derelict ex-Huddersfield trolleybuses, towed out to the course for race days from the municipal yard, and variously inscribed Ladies Toilet or Gentlemens Toilet. This purpose, though obviously serving a vital and necessary service, was possibly the most ignominious use to which secondhand buses have ever been applied.

There is – or was – a handy book called *Usage and Abusage* which instructs – or instructed – the reader in the art of writing good English. I like to hope that my

study of it has brought forth results in my contributions to *Classic Bus* and similar publications, and I carry a few additions to it in my mind in regard to transport, such as never describing a railway station as a train station and deploring the tautologous announcements all too frequently made nowadays on trains that the 'next station stop' will be Cheltenham or wherever the thing is next supposed to stop. I mean to say it isn't going to stop at some station slashed by the Beeching axe 30 years ago, is it! Equally on my blacklist is that the bus will leave at 'half four'. Having learnt German in my youth, long ago, I learnt also that *halb vier* (half four) means half *before* four or half past three, years before the offensive half-four gained a foothold in

common parlance. While I wonder how many hapless German travellers have waited an hour in England on this account, I am prepared to admit that my objection may be deemed pedantic, and I must admit also that I have dwelt upon the title of *Usage and Abusage* merely because I am borrowing it to suit the buses I am about to describe, for if Usage applies to their life in public service, Abusage may well fit what happens afterwards. A-bus-age . . . get it?

But perhaps it isn't all abuse and, having started in literary vein, I shall continue with a quotation from *As you like it*.

Sweet are the uses of adversity;
Which, like the toad, ugly and venomous,
Wears yet a precious jewel in his head:
And this our life exempt from public haunt
Finds tongues in trees, books in the running brooks,
Sermons in stones and good in every thing.
I would not change it.

I have always thought, actually, that Shakespeare was a bit unfair to the toad, surely a harmless and rather charming reptile. Be that as it may, I propose to add a B to the Bard's lines, thus Buses of Adversity, and then, if I carry on with *Bristols in Fairs, Bedfords in Hippie Camps, Trolleys as Loos and much abuse besides*, I am not straying too far from the original scansion and am prepared moreover to find jewels in the horny heads of all these nearly derelict buses. When a bus is no longer a bus it can start to claim a very forceful attraction . . .

Early date

The attraction caught me at an early date. When I was very young, in the late 1940s, I was taken sometimes to visit my mother's parents who lived at a place called Frilford a little west of Abingdon in what was then Berkshire. At this time the Atomic Energy Research Establishment at Harwell was in course of construction, and the labourers engaged in this work were conveyed to and from the scene of their labours

Top: *This delightful ex-Aberdeen 1937 Daimler COG6/Weymann, flanked by rather antiquated and ultra-modern in the private car line, was working for Bailey's, contractors, somewhere in the Poole area and is seen here parked at Fleet's Bridge, near Poole in 1962, give or take a year.*

Above: *A choice halfcab Maudslay serving as workmens' transport; but look again – what's wrong with the AEC? Yes, it's a mirror-image, for this is Lisbon in 1976; the AEC is one of many in the Lisbon Carris fleet and the Maudslay is one of several which formerly graced the Carris fleet in the days before Carris decided that it could have the cabs on its imported buses on what for it was the proper side of the bus.*

past Frilford. Quite why I know not, I can only assume they were housed somewhere west of Frilford, but I recall very well that to my great delight my father would take me out to the gate to view the convoy of buses serving for this transport. He pointed out that some of the buses were so old that they had open staircases at the back, and, that as many of the labourers were Irish they were wont to engage in fights, and such fights on the upper deck ended in precipitant descent of the stairs, open or otherwise. I have no recollection now of what the buses were, I seem to recall that some sported Corporation crests to which they were no longer entitled and to which my father called my attention, I suspect that the buses with open stairs were Leyland Titans. I am fairly sure, however, that those moments by the Frilford gate sowed the seeds for my lifelong (so far) devotion for buses not as buses. The buses of adversity . . .

Contractors always featured large in the abusage scene. After the Harwell episode, and when I had reached years of rather more discretion, in 1958 or 1959, I was able to identify the restroom of the lads working on the dual-carriagewaying of Barrack Road, Christchurch, then Hants, as a utility-bodied Bedford. I could not be so positive, however, about a little gem for British Railways' labourers sighted from the steam-hauled 'Hook Continental' *en route* for my first trip to

the continent in July 1958 but in my mind's eye I can see it still; it was a halfcab single-decker, among the sidings in some such place as Stratford, and conspicuous for being in the livery – already at that stage if I recall correctly on its way out – of railway carriage red and cream. Though this vehicle was obviously in use for the transit of toilers I am not sure if British Railways could be deemed contractors. In that period, however, I noted a lot of names of contractors, both great and small, who were using old buses, and from this almost Don Giovanni catalogue I here repeat a few: John Laing, Tersons, Furneaux, Faulkners, Thornycroft (Southampton), Dunning (Weyhill, Hants), Gleeson, Drewitt (Bournemouth), Turriff, Wimpey, Druce, Chivers, Dow-Mac (Tallington), and so on. Some were probably little jerry-builders, some were big boys and most have probably by now disappeared amidst bankruptcies or take-overs from the face of the very earth they were moving. So also, of course, have their buses, along with everything, so far as I am concerned, except the owners' names. For alas I took no details and very few photographs of what must surely have been in many cases specimens of choice antiquity.

It is probable that the contractors' buses suffered least in the realms of abusage, for they were still being used for human transport and, with the possible exception of the Harwell navvies, respectable at that. Another respectable form of adversity, respectable inasmuch as it was bus company operation, but far more detrimental to the vehicles, was conversion to tree-loppers and such like. My earliest acquaintance with victims of this ilk was the Bournemouth Corporation ex-Huddersfield AEC converted to tower wagon for the trolleybus overhead. I have mentioned this before in the pages of *Classic Bus Yearbook*, and also the sad fate of a couple of Bournemouth Guy Arab utilities which I remember perfectly well as buses and which suddenly emerged as a towing wagon and a trolleybus pole crane. Though it comes as a shock to see your friends thus mutilated I cannot deny that the results have an appeal of their own . . . Another cut-down Guy Arab was employed as a tree-lopper by King Alfred of Winchester, and to such effect that its use was banned by the council!

Respectable abuser

Another respectable abuser was the Regie Autonome des Transports Parisiens. Now although *Classic Bus* deals in the main with British-built buses the editor has allowed me before now to risk an excursion to my beloved Paris for neither he nor anyone else (or hardly) can deny that the celebrated Parisian open-rear platforms were some of the most classic buses ever. So

I shall hazard another excursion. If the reader recalls that the said buses were built not only with open rear platforms but also with open-sided cabs to which doors were added much later it will become instantly apparent that the conversion of such buses, especially the older specimens, to towing wagons or lorries produced some extremely bizarre spectacles.

Apart from using various buses for its own purposes the RATP engaged – and indeed still does – in a thriving traffic selling off the healthier of its withdrawn veterans for further use, and advertised the prewar Renaults as suitable for, among other purposes, school transport, mobile libraries, canteens, site offices, quarters for foremen or itinerant specialists or, with more drastic modification, transporters for compressors or grain dryers. They were on sale in the late 1960s for just over £300 a bus, but if you were inclined to buy 10 or more the price came down to £200. I have seen them myself serving as a tile transporter from a manufactury near Lyon, workmens' transport near Valenciennes, works canteen and another of less identifiable purpose on road widening in Brittany (with the intention of scrapping the narrow gauge railways) and, in Paris itself, as mobile cinema (not very long after I had ridden on that same bus in public service) or, permanently parked, as nightclub in the Rue Mouffetard and evangelical mission for the homeless on the quay near Austerlitz. And I have heard of them as fairground transport, Breton pancake shop, ski and skier transport in the French Alps, lampshade shop in Paris, fashion shop in Andorra and mobile beer hall (at least three) in Germany, to cite just a few. Naturally many also went for preservation, from Sweden to Spain (and points between) with up to a dozen in this country (of which, in case anybody doesn't know, I have four).

The charitable example on the quay near Austerlitz was remarkable not in itself but because it was part of a line of three parked

Above: *A Yorkshire Traction Leyland Tiger in splendidly abused form in Doncaster in 1961. This picture is, quite apart from the vehicular content, of some interest as it shows that Robert E. Jowitt in his early days made mistakes; the sun-blind on the shop behind appears almost to be an awning on the back of the bus!*

Left: *Miaow! The one on the left and the one above the cat's tail, at an RATP yard in the Parisian suburb of Pantin in 1970, are both Renault TN6As of 1932-3, at least if their bonnets and wheels are to be believed. The one on the left is more original in respect of mudguards and cab, the latter with doors added c1950, though the cab roof is a home-made inspiration to replace the canopy which would have come off with the body. The other vehicle has a TN4H 1936-7 windscreen and mudguards while roof and doors are quite ad hoc.*

end to end, the other two, extraordinarily enough, being an unidentified but typical Bristol and a completely identifiable Aldershot & District 1948 Dennis Lancet, last heard of previously in another form of abusage as a mobile shop in Spondon, Derbyshire. How on earth did these two end up as a home for the sleepers-under-the-bridges-of-Paris?

RT chip shop

Mind you, British buses ending up abroad are not unknown, but they are usually London buses. I have seen an RT working as a chip shop in the suburbs of Paris, and heard tell of others similarly employed. From the train outside Nevers, or was it Bourges(?), in 1989 I had a glimpse of one, though not a good enough glimpse to see if it was chip shop or something else; but the eye-catching quality of the well-known red London double-deck bus obviously lends itself to such pursuit. On the other hand. for many months in 1969-70 there was a grey London double-deck bus in a compound near the Normandy Ferry terminal in Le Havre. Again I can only ask: why?

Some London buses went abroad perfectly respectably to serve again as buses in places which were short of buses after the war, such as Belgium and Yugoslavia, but these, though in some cases they suffered much mutilation, were not being abused, so they are beyond my terms of reference, but I can allow myself to mention one which ended up as a Belgian agricultural shed. I hesitated to examine it closely because it was on the wrong side of a muddy field and also because I feared an irate Belgian landlord and also I did not wish to annoy the ladies with whom I was travelling, they having been halted already at frequent intervals for trams and trains; but it looked something like a Q, though with various odd features, but this might perhaps be expected after a spell as a Belgian bus and a perhaps even longer spell as a Belgian shed.

Sheds

The shed was another abuse, not only in Belgium, but also in England, where I dare say there were hundreds. For years there was one such between the villages of Ashley and Bashley in southern Hampshire. I lived near there when a teenager and saw it often, though only as we drove past it. My father, though always keen enough to rouse a complete stranger if he or she happened to have a derelict tram serving as shed, did not bother with buses, and I dare say I was too shy. By good luck I encountered and photographed this particular shed just after it had ceased to be a shed and was temporarily dumped on the side of the road on its way, I can only suppose, to the scrap heap. It was a delightful Thornycroft, perhaps originally a Bournemouth-London express coach. Another shed I often saw but never photographed was a utility Bedford in a shrubbery in the village of Downton not far south of Salisbury.

Just northwest of this same village, some way up a farm track, was another old single-decker, I know not

what, serving as a residence. I never got near this, nor near another serving the same purpose quite illegally in the New Forest near Cadnam. Again my father, though ever ready to fraternise with the inhabitants of dismounted railway carriages, considered that people who lived in derelict buses – and before the Town and Country Planning measures had effect there were plenty of them – were undesirable raggle-taggles much further down the social scale. Nevertheless, having frequently spotted from the train approaching Waterloo a colony of inhabited buses in a yard by the viaduct out of Victoria, I managed to make my way, not without difficulty, to what proved to be Havelock Terrace and to speak to the inhabitants who proved perfectly amiable if slightly Bohemian and said that one of the buses was an ex-Crosville Leyland. The other two, daubed in idyllic landscapes pre-dating the flower-power decoration of vehicles of swinging sixties days, were too Bohemian for recognition.

Top: *Perhaps the choicest snack bar of them all was this Dennis, previous history unknown, at Abergavenny bus station in 1960.*

Above: *An ex-Southdown Queen Mary Leyland PD3/Northern Counties in use as a hospitality or display bus, fights bravely against the evil of mankind and the indifference of picnicking racegoers at Epsom in the 1980s – long after the trolleybus loos had been scrapped, incidentally . . .*

Left: There are so many abuses for old buses that there was not room for all of them in the text, but here, taking up the playbus theme, is an earlier version of catering for children – though whether, when the children were lost, they knew where they had to go is debatable. Blackpool Corporation employed a couple of very Blackpool-style single-deckers, Burlingham-bodied Leyland Tigers, for the purpose. The lost child by the front wheel was Jowitt's sweetheart in 1964 (and has graced the pages of Classic Bus and Buses Annual before now). Sad to relate, Jowitt subsequently lost her . . .

Below: *The most glamorous, if perhaps the most mistreated, of all abused buses were surely those of the fairground. There is a thin dividing line between buses used as snack bars and buses selling food at fairs, but this example, a 1934 Western National Bristol J, ATT 822, with a 1949 Beadle body, falls definitely into the latter category. It has to be admitted that this photograph is a montage, irresistible because the two scenes went so well together, for the bus is at Queen's Park in Bournemouth in 1964 while the smoking mushes and the white-macintoshed birds are at the Southampton Common fair in 1961.*

My father likewise sped past Sarah's Snack Bar on the Great North Road near Scotch Corner but, on my protesting that Sarah's Snack Bar appeared highly meritorious, he promised that we would stop and inspect it next time we passed that way. Next time we passed that way Sarah's Snack Bar had become an ordinary hut, but Sarah directed us to a quarry in the neighbourhood where the former snack bar had been dumped. It was indeed meritorious, an ex-Darlington single-deck trolleybus of great though unguessable antiquity. Equally meritorious and sufficiently antique to impress my father – who didn't have to stop specially to see it for we were taking a morning walk round the town after staying in a hotel for the night – was a Dennis serving snacks in Abergavenny bus station.

Food and drink

The use of buses for selling food was a widespread form of abusage, though few examples were as choice as the two I have just described. The mobile shop which ended up in Paris was certainly only one among many serving in this role, though most if not all the others ended their days in British scrapyards. I

remember them but I do not remember taking much notice of them, and many buses serving as cafes did not at the time seem particularly noteworthy. A later generation of buses, an absolute spate of them, sprang up as roadside cafes in the 1970s and 1980s, and they did not seem noteworthy either, rather an eyesore, and I am not sure that even yet they would merit a place in *Classic Bus*. One or two which still survive might do soon! One travelling food-dispensing rarity was an RT, not because it was rare in itself but because most which survived went for preservation, but this was selling burgers. I came across it more than once, particularly selling burgers to yachtsmen at Cowes in Cowes Week, but it may well be that there are more RTs as snack bars abroad, as mentioned above, than there are in this country.

The giving away – rather than selling – of food and not infrequently drink also is known to involve old buses which travel to county shows and other popular assemblies where their owners dispense sustenance to their guests in the hope that the guests will purchase more of whatever it is that the owners are purveying, the bus serving the while as a fine large advertisement board for the owners and their services. I remember a

Southdown Queen Mary playing this role for some southern counties house agents and auctioneers. Another Queen Mary attending similar venues was perhaps less likely to dispense free bounty as it was calling attention either to the prevention of cruelty to animals or the prevention of illness in humans – I forget which – but obviously such charities cannot afford to dish out largesse. Only leaflets. Other double-deckers besides Queen Marys could and perhaps still can be encountered in these worthy pursuits. Yet another Queen Mary sat for many months outside a pub between Droitwich and Alcester, though if this one served food and drink it was probably not free, for the pub had its living to make. The bus was parked next to a large sailing boat, really large, probably twice as big as the bus. I passed this unlikely pair several times in the early 1990s and always intended to stop and photograph them, and never did, and then, like Sarah's Snack Bar, they had disappeared. Moving a Queen Mary might not prove a serious problem, but moving that boat would surely have been almost impossible. Still, there it was. Or wasn't. Another pub, the Seven Stars on the Winchester road outside Petersfield, boasted for a number of years an early Southampton Corporation Atlantean, painted grey. At the time it was perhaps hardly a classic bus, which, apart from laziness, was why I never stopped to photograph it. I have to hope that it was not in use for the sale of alcohol for its purpose appeared to be a children's playground.

The itinerant playbus rather than the pub garden playbus is a notion which though relatively new has been round long enough that the earlier specimens at least were halfcab, though later examples were and still are of flat front and less merit; so far! The idea of the playbus is that you fill the inside with sandpits and toys and paint the outside with gorillas and gnomes and take the result to schools and depressed areas to give the kids a change. While admiring those persons courageous enough to become involved in such a project I must admit it is a form of bus abusage which I would take some care to avoid. Let me return to the more heartening topics I was discussing before I became waylaid by gorillas . . .

If the RT provided a good chip shop on foreign shores the sale of chips in England – so far as these pages are concerned – was mainly conducted on single-deckers, and these generally though by no means invariably accompanied travelling fairs; and the buses employed by travelling showmen, not just for selling chips but as caravans and as general transport, may well have been the largest quantity and were certainly by far the most spectacular and colourful examples of abusage.

Showmen

The showmen were early in the field for derelict buses, for when petrol-electric buses were ousted by more modern methods of propulsion the showmen saw that in the victims of progress could be found a handy way of lighting their equipment; and then, once in the habit of buying secondhand buses, they kept on at it for many years. Of course they had ever an eye for a bargain, and whenever any trolleybus overhead wire was being replaced they knew by instinct or grapevine and were there to buy the discarded material for the purpose of earthing dodgem tracks. So the charms of cheap buses, even after the petrol-electric era, were not lightly denied, especially those of the Bristol L5G. This, though by all accounts a fairly dreadful vehicle from the passenger point of view with its noise and rough ride, was incredibly robust and promised to last almost for ever, even in the rugged terrain of the fairground and under the not necessarily gentle hands of showmen's employees. Some specimens of the Bristol L5G indeed lasted in this service until almost recent years, and in the height of the fairground bus era – at least as I remember it in the late 1950s and early 1960s – the Bristol was by far the most popular make in this role.

In the new age the natural successors to the fairground buses were the equally colourful and equally mutilated buses of the travellers or hippies. This example, complete with travellers, in its third existence, as dispensary for pancakes and coffee and simultaneously a hippie residence, had been in its second existence a racing car transporter after starting life in 1967 as an AEC Reliance/Plaxton with Premier of Preston.

The owner of this idyllic if decaying orchard at Upper Hill near Hereford has engaged in conflict with the local authorities for several years over his right to allow travellers to reside therein. At the time of writing this site is still there, though the population of buses varies. The Bristol MW has been re-registered – probably the original plate was sold at great price – but the destination blind may well be correct for origin as well as breed, though BOO is perhaps just fanciful. Other gems of antiquity lurk in the background in this January 1994 view.

Other makes abounded too, particularly Dennis, Leyland and AEC. But there were also a lot of rarities. And naturally there were never two vehicles alike, for every travelling showman was (and probably still is) an individualist and treated his bus according to his whims and his needs. Thus some of the buses, though gutted inside, looked from the outside much as they had looked in their bus life, while others were barely recognisable as buses, for example the halfcab luxury coach cut down to flat bed from one bay behind the cab . . . The most regular mutilation was to cut down the upper deck on double-deckers to just below window level, as this treatment provided useful space for the long poles required for the erection of side shows; nevertheless not a few double-deckers survived with the top deck intact. Or sort of! Liveries varied from the lurid red and yellow favoured by circuses through several earthy shades of maroon and brown and green to sundry greys and creams. Condition varied from utterly immaculate with chrome trimmings and decorations such as were never seen in psv days to not-fit-to-be-on-the-road with missing headlights and bald tyres. One way and another, a very paradise . . .

Furthermore these gaudy vehicles provided excellent excuse to visit travelling fairs for another form of worship. My mother, by force of habit rather than for any really good reason, would not have approved, had she known how well I esteemed it, of my conversation with and photography of the girls who attended travelling fairs. But, goodness, they were lovely! Few, perhaps, had true pre-Raphaelite or similar beauty, but, in the whiff of onions from the hot dog stalls and the sickly sweet stink of candy floss – and their own cheap perfume – and with the loud pounding blasting beat of Buddy Holly and of Cliff Richard in his unregenerate youth and Johnny Burnette – Girls, girls, pretty little girls, oh what they do to me – and the constant roar of old bus engines and sometimes the strident blast of the merry organ – formerly steam-driven – these pretty little girls with their fluffed-out bouffant hairstyles, their white macintoshes or raincoats which seemed the fashion even on the

sunniest evenings, their wide skirts supported by, presumably, a quantity of stiff petticoats giving way just above the knee to slim elegant legs ending in gold sandals or white stiletto heels, these girls had an allure which I have seldom if ever encountered since, and which is utterly lacking in the trainer-footed popular-sportwear-clad hoydens of today. Sandra, Terry, Jenny, Lynne (but Sandra most of all!) and never mind what my mother would have thought, when I think of the fairground buses of vanished days I think yet more fondly of you (and Sandra, little as you cared for me, most of all!).

And sometimes, when I was not too obsessed with the futile pursuit of Sandra – or even if I was – I would catch sight of brand new buses and wonder whether in some far distant future I would see them ending up as fairground transport in their turn.

Well, I never did, because a rising generation of showmen more or less entirely abandoned the practice of old buses, though I have had reports in the last few years of a Bristol FLF still travelling in this vein in Yorkshire, and have seen an ex-Plymouth Leyland double-deck employed by a fringe circus . . .

Nevertheless, the buses which were new in my Sandra youth have found an abusage as colourful and vagrant as the fairground buses of my teenage passions. Even as the last of the fairground buses faded away a new generation of travelling buses took to the roads, and in as gaudy a variety as those they replaced, in the hands of the peace convoys, the new-age travellers, the hippies, or any other media term

It is sometimes said that travelling showmen abandoned the use of secondhand buses when the skirts became too low. New age travellers were never worried by this, and if some took care not to enter places where skirt damage was likely, others either didn't care about the damage or else hacked off the skirts. This example is HHA 164L, a 1973 ex-Midland Red Ford R192/Plaxton Derwent, 21 years later!

you like. I think I have been accused of being a hippy myself for, when *en route* for Crich Extravaganza and urgently in need of adding more water before tackling the final mountains we pulled three Parisian Renaults into the first available layby and perforce by lack of space surrounded a Mini containing two elderly ladies, the two elderly ladies begged with some degree of terror to be let out forthwith. The ageing bus has become the trademark or token or emblem of the alternative – and to the respectable general public the not entirely desirable or decent – lifestyle.

Modified view

I may say that initially, being put to considerable pains and not inconsiderable expense to keep two or three 1930s Renaults on the road legally with MoT certificates and insurance and tax, I was totally opposed to the hippies who could and apparently would run elderly buses without any of these prerequisites. I have subsequently, after studying the hippies and their buses in some depth, had occasion to modify such a view. For example, while it is obviously deplorable and quite illegal to run a vehicle untaxed, uninsured and without an MoT certificate, any one or more of these crimes are such as several of our friends or acquaintances or next-door neighbours are engaging in occasionally or sometimes or often, yes, your friends and next-door neighbours too!

Secondly, while the bus enthusiast will say that the hippy wrecks his bus – and in some cases there is some truth in this, such as cutting off the entire back of a double-decker and rebodying it one bay shorter presumably to make it more Glastonbury-terrain friendly, or for the same purpose to hack off the back of a Bedford VAL or to strip off the skirts of a perhaps ex-Midland Red – the hippy may reasonably argue that if he did not keep the bus in whatever form it would otherwise be scrapped. And in many instances, if not too free with the hacksaw, the new age traveller is very aware of the intrinsic value of his bus, which also happens to be his home, or, in some cases, her home, painstakingly decorated with elaborate Celtic motifs or rainbow visions. Moreover the bus has frequently been rescued from some other interim form of abusage, two such in recent decades being carriage of majorettes and transport of racing cars; and while you may argue

that the carriage of majorettes is no worse and indeed rather more dainty than the carriage of hob-nail-booted sons of toil the conversion of a Bedford VAL to a racing car transporter is probably far more drastic, being backed by finance and wrought by equipment both out of reach of the average traveller, so it must be said that many hippy buses are now no worse off than they were then. I will not here dwell on the rest of the accusations against new age travellers such as dole-scrounging, keeping of ill-disciplined dogs and even more undisciplined children, and a catalogue of other crimes as long as my list of contractors' buses, most of which charges could equally and in some cases with more reason be levelled against other sections of the population. Suffice it to say that the new age traveller's bus, be it a horrible Moseley body which deserves no better than to be cut up to allow a touring caravan to be sewn into its middle or be it a Bedford Duple Vega in almost original condition – except for the ethnic-scarfed vegetarian interior – is a worthy successor to the now much valued and often more mistreated showman's bus, and, due to perhaps over-heavy political and media discrimination, liable to become more rapidly extinct.

Such, however, is plainly the lot of all buses in abusage. Extinction . . . or preservation. And is there much to choose between them? Dare I suggest, to editorial and readership gasps of horror, that the buses of adversity, from transporters of labourers and fairground gear to hippy homes and even humble Derby Day toilets, were serving a more real or valid purpose than are the buses in preservation? This is in no way intended to deride or dismiss the efforts of bus preservers, whose efforts have in truth brought much pleasure to me and many others; and I would not be without my beloved Parisian Renaults, but how much have I saved from the streets of Paris as I remember them in the 1960s? Is it any more real a memory than the memory of the grey-eyed enigmatic long-lasting never-to-be-deciphered look which Sandra gave me one summer evening in 1960 while Frank Ifield shouted 'On the level I'm a lucky devil to find a little angel like you' and in the background some Dennis or Bristol throbbed endlessly and patiently in usage and abusage, unknowingly awaiting oblivion . . ? **CB**

CLASSIC
WONDER
BUS

ALAN MILLAR's Classic Blunderbus column in *Classic Bus* magazine looks at bus and coach models that never quite made it, for a variety of reasons. As an antidote, the Yearbook offers you an unlikely Wonderbus candidate

SENSUAL ENTERTAINMENT may not be words you expect to read in a book such as this, but I suggest they describe one reason why many of us enjoy travelling by bus. For unlike the vast majority of passengers whose fares make or break an operator's routes and for whose benefit bus services must run, we're not always so fussed about getting from A to B as we are about enjoying the experience of the journey itself. Our senses are entertained and that's partly why I believe that the Guy Arab was one of the British bus industry's all-time greats.

I won't very likely admit this in mixed company, but get me aboard an Arab – and especially a MkIV with manual gearbox and Gardner 6LW engine – and my ears will be in seventh heaven. Something in the combination of all the bits of drivetrain put together by

Guy and its suppliers created a whining low gear melody hard to equal in my memory. Yes, Mozart could do better, but within the bounds of what can be achieved by automotive engineers, Fallings Park, Wolverhampton brought music to my ears.

Now people may tell you – and, whisper it, they might be right – that the whines evoking all this passion were a product of inefficiency you would never get in the likes of one of today's quiet, lowfloor, low emission, fully automatic citybuses. But such failings can be excused. And I excuse them in the same way as I let a different set of tuneful sounds sweep away all thoughts of the deficiencies in the mid-1950s diesel multiple-units providing my local train service as I write this article in January 1999.

People who have driven Arabs will also testify to the hard work and discomfort of driving them day-in, day-out in urban service. I don't doubt their stories, but they won't destroy by belief that this was a very special and successful breed of bus. Indeed, in those moments when I dream up my own fantasy bus fleet, reality goes right out of the window as a batch or more of crash gearbox Arab IVs makes it into imagined front-line service, howling magically into the night as they climb invisible hills.

Fondly recalled

My case, I should make clear, isn't just founded on fondly recalled sensual entertainment. There are hard facts, too. While I know I would be exaggerating in the extreme to say that the Arab won World War 2 for Britain, this remarkable bus's reputation was made by the important part it played in helping make the war machine function – and its role as the wartime bus sowed the seeds for successful sales for another 20 years and more.

Had it not been for the ambitions of Adolf Hitler and Britain's determination to put an end to his plans for world domination, the Arab would have merited little more than a footnote in the history of 20th century British buses. Guy was a marque too many for the double-deck market in the 1930s which fast became dominated by Leyland, AEC, Daimler and Bristol, with the likes of Dennis, Crossley and Albion filling most remaining gaps.

The Arab had broken new ground when first launched in 1933 as – allegedly – the first double-deck chassis available only with a diesel engine. But demand was weak and Guy struggled while its rivals prospered. Southampton Corporation – significantly as later events would reveal – showed more faith than most by acquiring 11, and Burton-upon-Trent continued to take single-deck Arabs into the early months of the war. But the Wolverhampton manufacturer seemed about as relevant to the needs of prewar British fleets as people like Quest 80 would half a century later.

Fate

Then fate changed everything. Bus manufacture was halted to make way for military needs, especially after the army found itself abandoning equipment on the occupied side of the Channel as our forces were evacuated through Dunkirk in 1940. A little later, when the initial panic eased and bus fleets pressed for new buses to be built, central government took charge

Swindon Corporation received some of the earliest utility Guy Arabs, like No 48 (CWV 375) of 1942 seen here, with Park Royal 56-seat body. It was the second utility Arab chassis to be built.
Roy Marshall

and placed an initial order for 1,000 standard, basic double-deckers for service around the country.

Guy, one name least likely to have figured on anyone's tendering list, was suddenly in an excellent position to play a pivotal part in reinventing the British bus. The story goes that it lost an order for searchlight trailers when cleverer aircraft detection technology became available and was selected to build 500 of those first 1,000 buses.

Leyland was to have built the others, but was diverted on to military work, and the idea seems to have been to try and standardise at least some of the componentry. But for a manufacturer with little real clout in the bus market, Guy exercised a surprising amount of influence when it was suggested that it build something close to Bristol's established K5G. It was having none of it, and instead adapted the 1933 Arab to make use of available materials and to meet some of the tighter dimensional constraints laid down from on high.

The resulting chassis, I guess, was the equivalent of someone decreeing that only a modified Ailsa or Leyland Leopard could be supplied for mainstream operation in 1999. It was a competent design, but nowhere near the leading edge in bus engineering. Yet, while it may have been outdated by the standards of the day, over 2,500 were built between 1941 and 1946, with 435 going to London Transport which, as far as anyone knows, never even looked at a Guy bus catalogue before. Birmingham, which had bought a solitary Arab in 1934, took 84.

Exceptional times

In those exceptional times before peacetime manufacturing resumed at Leyland and AEC, the utility Arab was Britain's best-selling double-decker. It could have fizzled out again as rapidly as it rose from obscurity, but its honest-to-goodness simplicity and reliability persuaded many fleets to go on buying its slightly more sophisticated successors in surprisingly large quantities.

Such was its impact that, after the utility's five-year production run ended, Guy went on to build Arabs for another 24 years, selling around as many MkIII, IV and V models on the home market as the utility models known either officially or unofficially as MkIs and IIs. That business was supplemented by export sales, notably in Africa and Asia. The last 12 Arab Vs went to China Motor Bus in Hong Kong in 1970, were followed by front-engined Guy-built Leyland Victory double-deckers which might well never have sold had the Arab not been developed, and CMB later had Arabs rebodied for long-term service.

At home, some of its biggest triumphs were with municipal fleets. Perhaps there was no great surprise that Wolverhampton supported its local manufacturer to the tune of 246 Arab III, IV and V models, including some with the relatively rare specifications of Meadows and AEC engines. Or that nearby Walsall took 40 Arab IIIs.

But a huge success – unthinkable before the war – was Birmingham's purchase of 301 of the first Arab IVs (a model developed around this major fleet's requirements) as part of its massive investment of tram replacement buses. They operated alongside 501 similar 'new look' Daimlers and 100 Crossleys.

Proportionately, Southampton went even further, making a massive postwar investment in 185 Arab IIIs, the last of which arrived four years after Birmingham's first Arab IV. Burton continued its prewar loyalty right up until 1962/3 when – under Jaguar ownership – Guy began phasing out 27ft Arab production in favour of Daimlers with manual gearboxes.

Other conquests

The many other conquests included batches of Arab IIIs and IVs for Edinburgh (which also bought 60 of the London utilities for rebodying), and IVs and Vs for Cardiff and Chester. Indeed, Chester bought the last UK market Arab of all in 1969 when half-cabs were finally disappearing from manufacturers' catalogues.

There were many more, spread from Belfast to South Shields, Exeter to Accrington. And company fleets were tempted, too. Within the BET empire, Midland Red took 20 Meadows-powered Arab IIIs and no more, but there was far more of a following in fleets like Northern General and Southdown, even though they continued to buy Leylands as well. On the other hand, East Kent broke completely with its past loyalty to Leyland in 1950, taking 135 Arab IIIs and IVs before turning to AEC in the late-1950s. The Scottish Bus Group bought over 240 Arab IIIs and IVs as well as relieving London Transport of 132 utilities.

Guy also did well among independents. West Riding bought 70 Arab IVs before persuading Guy to develop the downright disastrous but technically ambitious Wulfrunian. Lancashire United tried one Wulf, but returned to the Arab to the extent that a succession of over 260 MkIII, IV and V models formed the backbone of its fleet right up to the end of its independence. The Red & White group would most likely have bought Arabs by the crate load, too, had it not sold out to the British Transport Commission in 1950 while Duple-bodied Arab III double-deckers were going into its fleets.

It would be wrong to say the Arab was the best or most refined double-decker of its day, but it was a well-designed, uncomplicated machine which stood favourable comparison with most of its rivals. Wartime familiarity helped it gain rapid access to a cross-section of the industry which was impressed enough to buy it in big numbers.

And it sounded like nothing on earth. **CB**

The Corporation fleet in Wolverhampton, Guy's home town, was a natural Arab customer. This 1957 Arab IV with Metro-Cammell Orion 60-seat body, No 11 (SUK 11), had a Gardner 6LW engine and, unusually, a preselector gearbox.

CONNECTIONS

G. H. TRURAN explores the connections between aircraft manufacture and bus bodybuilding, and looks particularly at the products of Saunders and Saunders-Roe

The first Saunders Rivaloy double-deck body was built on this reconditioned Maidstone & District Bristol K5G chassis.
All photos from SEAS, Saunders and Saunders-Roe collections

FOR MANY YEARS there existed a relationship between the aircraft and passenger vehicle operating industry and names such as Short Bros, Scottish Aviation, Bruce Coachworks of Cardiff and Marshall's of Cambridge come to mind.

In the case of Short Bros, the decline in orders for aircraft at the end of World War 1 brought about a need to find alternative work for the factory at Rochester, coupled with a requirement to keep a skilled workforce in employment until new aircraft could be designed and put into production. To meet these needs, Short Bros turned to the design and production of public service vehicle bodywork, starting with an initial order from London General, which was in need of a lightweight double-deck bus body with an increased seating capacity, within the existing front and rear axle loadings of the time. The new body carried an extra five persons over existing designs and eventually over 2,000 bodies of this type were supplied. Similar bodies were built for Tillings. When Short Bros

were taken over by the Government in 1943, Sir Frederick Heaton, as he was to become, from the Tilling Group, became chairman of Short Bros; the firm was by then engaged in the production of Sunderland flying boats and Stirling heavy bombers for the war effort.

In a period of some 15 years Short Bros became a major supplier of coachwork to BET Group companies such as Devon General, Midland Red, Maidstone & District, Southdown and municipal undertakings such as Birmingham, Hull and Nottingham. Production of bodywork at Rochester continued until 1935, when the need for aircraft arose and the skilled bodymakers transferred over to aircraft production.

In a similar way after the end of World War 2, other

A completed AEC Regal MkI for Northern General with a BEF-style Saunders body, an early order for complete rather than refurbished bodies.

One of the Foden PVSC chassis bodies by Saunders and supplied to Green Bus of Rugeley.

firms previously engaged in the aircraft industry were looking for other avenues of work, again to keep both their factories and workforces employed. Scottish Aviation entered the public service vehicle body manufacturing industry, using its expertise in the use of aluminium alloys in the construction and repair of aircraft in the design and construction of single- and double-deck bus and coach bodies, although unlike Short Bros, it was not engaged in the business for any length of time.

Bruce Coachworks of Cardiff was another firm which in prewar years had been engaged in the aircraft industry, operating a courier service between Croydon airport and the continent. In the early years of World War 2 it relocated to Cardiff, to become involved in the repair and maintenance of aircraft at Cardiff airport. At the end of the war, Air Dispatch, as the firm was titled, found itself looking for alternative work, and started to refurbish public service vehicle bodies for operators in South Wales and other areas,

the work including refurbishment of trolleybus bodies for St Helens Corporation. Building on this work, an agreement was entered into with East Lancashire Coachbuilders of Blackburn to assemble bodywork to its design for operators in the South Wales area, with the principal customer being Cardiff Corporation. Over the years bodywork was supplied to Newport Corporation, Bedwas & Machen Urban District Council, Llanelly & District Traction, The Swan Motor Services of Swansea, Green's Motors of Haverfordwest, The West Monmouthshire Omnibus Board, Gelligaer Urban District Council and to the municipal undertakings of Accrington, Rotherham, Warrington and Eastbourne; the very last bodies were supplied to Eastbourne in 1951 when the factory, now titled Bruce Coachworks, was closed.

Motor dealers

Marshall's of Cambridge started as motor dealers, expanding into the aircraft industry between the two

world wars through the provision of an airport in Cambridge, a flying school and the repair and maintenance of aircraft. Subcontract work was also carried out, as it still is today, with the nose section of Concorde being manufactured by the company. At the end of World War 2, Marshall's started to refurbish bodywork for London Transport and this, together with the later purchase of Mulliner's, led to the creation of the Omnibus Division within the company. Much of Mulliner's production had been exported, as had Marshall's. In the early 1960s production of a single-deck bus body to BEF design was started, being supplied to most BET Group companies and also to some municipalities, making the company one of the leading suppliers of bodywork to the BET Group, until the advent of the National Bus Company and the Leyland National single-deck bus. With the decline in orders received from NBC, production of public service vehicle bodies at Cambridge tailed off until a double-deck bus body was designed and put into production, with the first examples being supplied to Leicester City Transport on Dennis Dominator chassis and other similar examples going to Derby Borough Transport, again on Dennis Dominator chassis. Other double-deck bodies were supplied on Leyland

Top: *The first Saunders double-deck body supplied to Southdown, mounted on a reconditioned 1938 Leyland Titan TD5 chassis in 1947.*

Above: *The first, and only, Saunders double-deck bodies built for export were on AEC Regent MkIII for Durban, South Africa. Here six are nearing completion, with AEC Regal MkIIIs for Lisbon to the left of the photo.*

Atlantean AN68 chassis to South Yorkshire PTE, on Scania chassis to Newport Transport and on Leyland Olympian chassis for Bournemouth Corporation. One Scania chassis was bodied as a demonstration bus, seeing initial service in Ireland. Other double-deck bodies were supplied on Volvo Ailsa B55 and Citybus chassis for the Greater Glasgow PTE and Derby City Transport. Production of public service vehicle bodywork continues at Cambridge to this day.

Saunders

Another company involved in the aircraft industry prior to World War 2 was Saunders-Roe, who commenced bodywork production at the end of the war. The roots of this company lay in shipbuilding, although it had become involved in the design and production of aircraft during World War 1.

S. E. Saunders, as the company was titled, was based on the Isle of Wight. The aircraft side of the business was not profitable although the company became linked with Short Bros through subcontract work on flying boats. With the outbreak of war, the company relocated to a new factory at Beaumaris on the Isle of Anglesey. Here work centred on the preparation of Catalina flying boats for service with the British armed forces, these having flown over from North America. Again at the end of the war, this company faced the problem of keeping its workforce employed in an area of high unemployment. The shipbuilding yard on the Isle of Wight had been destroyed during the war and with the transfer of the aircraft design section back to Cowes it was decided to restart ship building at Beaumaris, with the company being retitled Saunders Engineering & Shipyard Company. Work started on refurbishing public service vehicle bodywork with single- and double-deck buses and coaches being received from Northern General, Southdown, United Auto and Southern Vectis. Whilst this work was in progress, design work on a single-deck bus body was under way. An order for single-deck bus bodies to BEF design was received from Northern General, the bodies to be mounted on AEC Regal MkI chassis. Other single-deck bus bodies were supplied on Foden PVS and Guy Arab MkIII chassis, whilst one single-deck bus body, again to BEF design,

Above: *Left-hand drive ACLO Regal MkIIIs with 37-seat Saunders bodies for Sao Paulo.*

Left: *The first Rivaloy single-deck body fitted to a reconditioned prewar Leyland Tiger chassis for Crosville.*

was supplied to Northern General on a reconditioned Leyland Tiger chassis. The Balfour Beatty company, Midland General, took delivery of single-deck bus bodies mounted on Leyland Tiger PS1 chassis, which were very similar to Weymann bodies of the period. Double-deck bodies on reconditioned Leyland Titan chassis were supplied to Southdown. The first and only Saunders double-deck bodies built for export were supplied on long-wheelbase AEC Regent MkIII chassis to Durban Corporation, South Africa.

In the early years, most of the bodies designed and produced at Beaumaris used body sections designed and patented by Short Bros in prewar years, until the introduction of the Rivaloy range of designs. The last double-deck bus bodies built to the Saunders-Short Bros designs were supplied to Maidstone & District, mounted on Bristol K6A chassis.

Export orders

Export orders dominated production at Beaumaris in the early postwar years, with bodies to Dutch design being supplied on left-hand drive long-wheelbase Guy Arab MkIII chassis for service in Holland. Single-deck bus bodies to meet the requirements of Lisbon Electric Tramways were supplied on left-hand drive AEC Regal MkIII chassis, either as complete vehicles or as body shells for completion in the operator's workshop. Other single-deck bus bodies mounted on left hand drive ACLO Regal MkIII chassis were supplied to Buenos Aires Transport Board; these had full fronts surrounding the radiator. Similar single-deck bus bodies were supplied to Sao Paulo, again mounted on ACLO Regal MkIII left-hand drive chassis, although these bodies were given a redesigned full front which concealed the radiator.

Left: **A Daimler CVD6 chassis with Rivaloy body for Kumasi Municipal Transport, Gold Coast.**

Below: Ten left-hand drive Leyland Royal Tiger chassis with Rivaloy bodies await shipment to Cuba.

Left: *The attractive Saunders-Roe Saro body mounted on Leyland Tiger Cub for East Midland, part of the BET order.*

Below: *BUT RETB1 trolleybuses for Auckland, New Zealand, the only trolleybuses built by Saunders-Roe, are collected from Beaumaris by Leyland service lorries. Rivaloy bodies were also supplied to Auckland on Bedford SB, Daimler Freeline and Leyland Royal Tiger motorbus chassis.*

A major order was received from London Transport for double-deck bus bodies to be mounted on AEC Regent MkIII chassis. This order caused Saunders to redesign its double-deck body to meet the requirements of London Transport, although the Saunders-Short pillar sections were used in their construction. A new body design was introduced known as the Rivaloy for both double- and single-deck use, the first examples of the single-deck design being supplied to Crosville Motor Services on reconditioned Leyland Tiger chassis. Similar bodies were supplied to the Lincolnshire Road Car Company on reconditioned AEC Regal chassis. Two Rivaloy single-deck bodies were mounted on Commer Avenger chassis for use as demonstration vehicles and these were the first bodies to carry the deep, rounded, 'American'-style front dome, which was to become a distinctive Saunders/Saunders-Roe/Saro body feature. The first

examples of the Rivaloy single-deck body were designed for front-engined chassis, but it was soon redesigned for fitment to underfloor-engined chassis. Rivaloy single-deck bus bodies mounted on Daimler CVD6 chassis were exported to the Gold Coast for use by Kumasi Municipal Transport.

The first Rivaloy double-deck bus body was mounted on a reconditioned Bristol K5G chassis to the order of Maidstone & District.

The first large orders for the Rivaloy single-deck bus body were received from Cuba, all to be mounted on left-hand drive Leyland Royal Tiger chassis, to be supplied in a mix of completed vehicles, or in partially knocked-down (pkd) form for assembly in Cuba. Completed vehicles were shipped with three chassis to which had been fitted floors and step pans, upon which were loaded body sides, roof sections, front and rear

The experimental Leyland Lowloader rear-engined double-decker, later registered STF 90, at Beaumaris soon after completion. It will be seen that many Saro body parts were used in its construction. The O.350 engine was mounted on the rear platform, and the engine cover can just be seen.

domes, seats and other fittings in boxes, sufficient parts to complete three bodies, A similar body, again mounted on a left-hand drive Leyland Royal Tiger chassis was supplied to the Anglo-Iranian Oil Company, fitted with wooden slatted three-and-two seating. A Cuba-style body was also supplied to an undertaking in Miami, again mounted on a left-hand drive Leyland Royal Tiger chassis. Similar buses were supplied to the Compania Uraguaya de Transportes Collectives SA and also to the Argentine Government.

All-aluminium

Development work continued on the double-deck Rivaloy design and a lightweight all-aluminium alloy version was fitted to an AEC Regent MkIII chassis for experimental and demonstration purposes in 1951. The bus was to enter service for a short period of time with Maidstone & District before being sold to a member of the AA Service co-operative.

Leyland Royal Tiger chassis were also supplied to Irish operators, but in this case the bodies were supplied in shell form for completion in the operators' own workshops. Erne Bus, Londonderry & Lough Swilly Railway, the Great Northern Railway and the Irish Republic Army, all received bodies in this fashion.

In 1951 the company was retitled Saunders-Roe (Anglesey) Ltd confirming the link with the Isle of Wight-based Saunders-Roe company.

Development work continued on the single-deck Rivaloy design, with the introduction of an all-aluminium alloy version for use on the recently-introduced Leyland Tiger Cub chassis, which was to become known as the 'Saro' body. Saunders-Roe received an order for the supply of this body, all to be mounted on Leyland Tiger Cub chassis, as part of an order placed by the BET Group for 500 of these chassis. Saunders-Roe supplied bodies to Ribble, Yorkshire Traction, East Midland, Trent, Thomas Bros (Port Talbot), Northern General and Sunderland District. Other Leyland Tiger Cub chassis were bodied by Saunders-Roe for Leyland Motors, to be used as demonstration buses, seeing service with London Transport, the Ulster Transport Authority and by Christchurch Transport, New Zealand (the latter being the sole dual-doored Saro body).

A single Saro lightweight double-deck bus body was supplied on a Guy Arab chassis to satisfy the requirements of Birmingham City Transport and the completed vehicle was displayed on the Saunders-Roe stand in the 1952 Commercial Motor Show.

A further lightweight Saro double-deck body, mounted on a reconditioned AEC Regal chassis, was supplied to Devon General. A major export order was received from the Auckland Transport Board for the supply of Rivaloy single-deck bus bodies to be mounted on Leyland Royal Tiger, Daimler Freeline, Bedford SB and BUT RETB1 trolleybus chassis. These were the only trolleybus chassis bodied by Saunders-Roe. As with the Cuba order the Auckland order called for the majority of the bodies to be supplied in pkd form for assembly in Auckland, although as before some bodies were completed in Anglesey, either painted in the operator's livery or in grey primer.

A small batch of Rivaloy bodies were supplied to Kumasi Municipal Transport, all mounted on Daimler Freeline chassis.

A single Saro body was supplied to Guy Motors, mounted on the Guy Arab LUF underfloor-engined chassis for use as a demonstration vehicle. As built the vehicle was finished in the livery of Northern General, to whom it was first demonstrated.

One other Saro single-deck bus body was fitted to the integral single-deck bus developed by Saunders-Roe. Powered by a Gardner 5HLW engine, driving through a David Brown gearbox, the completed vehicle was extensively tested at the MIRA test ground before entering service with Maidstone & District. The weight saving was not as much as anticipated with this design and this vehicle remained the sole example. This, with the Guy demonstrator, were the sole examples of Saro single-deck bus bodywork not to be fitted to a Leyland Tiger Cub chassis.

Lowloader

In 1953 an all-aluminium double-deck bus body was supplied to Leyland Motors, fitted to the experimental Leyland Lowloader rear-engined double-deck chassis. As it was a one-off body, many parts from the single-deck Saro body were used in its construction. Used as a demonstration vehicle by Leyland before being sold to Lowland Motorways, the vehicle was the forerunner of the Leyland Atlantean chassis.

Two final Saro lightweight double-deck bodies, mounted on AEC Regent MkIII chassis, were supplied in 1954 to Liverpool City Transport. Manufactured to resemble the Crossley double-deck bodies, supplied as part of an order for 100 buses, One of the Saunders-Roe bodies was supplied to Liverpool in an unpainted aluminium finish.

With the completion of the last of the second order for single-deck bus bodies placed by Auckland Transport, all mounted on Daimler Freeline chassis, in 1956, body design and production came to an end at Beaumaris. Production concentrated on Ministry of Defence projects.

In 1968, by which time the company had become part of the Laird Group and re-titled Cammell-Laird (Anglesey) Ltd, production of public service vehicle bodywork was restarted at Beaumaris. MCW-designed and manufactured bodies were assembled on to Leyland Titan PD3 and Atlantean chassis for Brighton Corporation and Devon General. These were followed by the assembly of Superior Coach Company body kits on to Ford and Bedford chassis. The Laird Group having taken a licence to import body kits and supply completed vehicles for use in the United Kingdom and Europe.

These were to be the last passenger-carrying bodies completed at the Beaumaris factory, although refuse collection vehicle and road-gritting bodies continued to be built at the plant.

In many ways, Saunders-Roe was an innovative company, particularly in the use of aluminium in the construction of its bodies and in the unique method devised for the supply of pkd bodies, particularly for the export market. Orders for large numbers of bodies could only be satisfied through the extensive use of body jigs, where again Saunders-Roe was a leader in their use. This was a particular feature in obtaining export orders.

Examples of Saunders and Saunders-Roe bodywork may still be seen, some overseas remain in everyday service, whilst others are owned and cared for by preservationists in this country. **CB**

Chassis Code Cracking

In each issue of *Classic Bus* magazine, GEOFF BURROWS explains the complexities of the codes given by bus and coach manufacturers to their chassis. In the Yearbook he turns his attention to one of the most prolific manufacturers

BEDFORD

From the introduction of the Bedford range in 1931, bus and coach chassis were derived from equivalent truck chassis, and used the same designations, with the addition of the letter B. The first was the WHB, a normal control model with 3.18-litre six cylinder engine and 10ft 11in wheelbase (w/b) chassis suitable for 14-seat bodies. A 13ft 1in w/b version soon appeared; the WLB could carry 20 seats. Demand for a larger vehicle led to some WTL lorry chassis being fitted with 25-seat coach bodies. In 1935 the WTB replaced the WLB; this had semi-forward control arrangement, this time with 13ft 11in w/b for 26-seat bodies. A new 3.519-litre engine was used in the WTB from 1938, and at the same time the radiator and bonnet assembly were given a new appearance. In mid-1939 the OB replaced the WTB. It utilised the same engine and gearbox in a lower-height 14ft 6in w/b chassis, which was easily recognised by the completely new style of radiator grille. Production ceased almost immediately but was resumed in 1942 as the OWB. Apart from the lack of brightwork, the chassis was virtually unchanged, unless you consider small wartime headlamps and absence of aluminium alloy in the construction. Although the OB was designed for 26 seats, the wartime version carried 32, and when reintroduced in 1946 the standard became 29.

The OB was replaced in 1950 by the SB, a forward control 17ft 2in w/b model with a new Bedford 4.9-litre six cylinder petrol engine. Seating 33, the model was reclassified in 1953 when diesel power was offered. The SBO (oil) was supplied with Perkins R6 diesel; the SBG (gasoline) was the new designation for the SB. In 1955 the wheelbase was increased to 18ft 0in to allow a 30ft long body which could carry 41 seats. From 1959 suffix numbers replaced the letters identifying the engines. The range eventually became SB1 – Bedford Diesel 4.59 litres; SB3 – Bedford Petrol 4.59 litres; SB5 – Bedford Diesel 5.049 litres; SB8 – Leyland Diesel 350 cu in; SB13 – Leyland Diesel 370 cu in.

A new range of bus chassis appeared in the 1960s, these were not derived from truck chassis so that 'B' was no longer a feature of the codes. The VA range had vertical front engines with setback front axles allowing front entrances on longer models. VAS was short wheelbase, VAM medium and the VAL was long wheelbase with two front steering axles. Additional engines to the range previously noted were 2 - Bedford 214cu in petrol, 14 - Leyland 401cu in diesel, and 70 - Bedford 7.6-litre.

In 1968, Bedford introduced computer coding for all parts and schedules. Chassis were given a seven-character code. It was normally only necessary to use the first three characters to identify bus chassis, but we will explain the full system because in some circumstances the complete code was needed.

1st character	Model line
2nd character	Engine
3rd character	Gross Vehicle Weights
4th character	Wheelbase
5th character	Transmission and Rear Axle
6th & 7th characters	Cab or body detail

1. Model Line

N	Formerly	SB
P	Formerly	VAS
T	Formerly	VAM (T was later altered to B)
W	Formerly	VAL
Y	The new mid-engined range	
J	The new midi-bus	

2. Engine

O	All engines appropriate to the model line
D	214 cu in Petrol
F	300 cu in Petrol
J	330 cu in Diesel
R	466 cu in Diesel
L	8.2-litre Diesel derated to 110kW power
M	8.2-litre Diesel 119kW or Turbocharged to 130kW
N	8.2-litre Diesel Turbocharged to 153kW power

3. Gross Vehicle Weights

O	All appropriate GVW
J	Approx 8,000kg
K	Approx 7,000kg
M	Approx 9,900kg
P	Approx 10,400kg
Q	Approx 11,400kg
T	Approx 13,000kg
V	Max 16,000kg

4. Wheelbase

O	All appropriate wheelbases
I	Short wheelbase
2	Medium wheelbase
3	Long wheelbase
4	Extra long wheelbase

5. Transmission and Rear Axle

O	All appropriate options
B	four-speed gearbox, single-speed axle
D	five-speed gearbox, single-speed axle
N	six-speed gearbox, single-speed axle
R	Automatic transmission, single-speed axle
V	six-speed overdrive gearbox, single-speed axle

6. Cab and Body Detail

This character consists of two letters, used to indicate the factory-fitted structure needed to enable the chassis to be driven short distances, where appropriate. These temporary structures, which were not 'road legal', were then removed. This character also covered other possible cab or body options.

OO	All appropriate options
ZO	Temporary drive-away front end
EO	Drive-away front end with mostly permanent content
KO	Ready-to-run integral bus

In the early 1980s new international regulations governing such matters as Vehicle Identification Numbers (VIN) were introduced, and they banned the use of letters O and Q. Thus the seventh letter of the code was deleted, and model YMQ was re-designated YMP. If you try to read the chassis number stamped on the frame, you will find that the first three letters are SKF. These identify the manufacturer and country of origin.

As will have been noticed, these codes cover the new Y range introduced in the early 1970s. These were vertical mid-engined chassis, the YRQ replaced the VAM in 1970, and the YRT replaced the VAL in 1972. The new codes caused the VAS to be re-classified PJK, and even the SB was changed to NJM. The last new Bedford passenger chassis was introduced in 1984, the 12m YNV. This was unique in that it was given a name, Venturer. The JJL midibus will also have been noticed, built in 1978. The full code would have been JJL1RKO.

Due to the close association between truck and passenger chassis, there have been many examples of bus and coach bodies fitted to truck chassis. Most of these are beyond the scope of this feature, but we will give as examples the WLG used for 14-seat buses in 1938, and the J2 which had a Caetano 20-seat coach body designed for it in the 1970s.

Finally, it is believed that the Bedford name, chosen by the American owners of the company, General Motors, referred to a previous model in their range, the Bedford Buick. **CB**

This article would not have been possible without the detailed help provided by Leo J. Taylor of Dunstable, to whom we extend our grateful thanks.

Above: *A 1978 line-up posed to mark the production of 3million Bedfords since 1931. A 1931 14-seat WHB TM 9347, the very first Bedford bus, with Waveney body, is flanked by YRTs for Eastern National (left, with Duple Dominant II body) and Albanian (right, with Plaxton Supreme).*

Right: *Bedford's main passenger models in the years 1935-9 was the WTB, here seen with 25-seat Duple KD Special body for Orange Luxury Coaches, complete with externally-mounted spare wheel.*

FROM
JOHN SMITH'S ALBUM

ALAN TOWNSIN takes a further dip into the photographs of another distinguished former *Buses Illustrated* editor

A S WITH the previous selection, published in *Classic Bus 13*, these photographs come from the 1952-53 period, when E. J. Smith was working in AEC's publicity department at Southall, as well as editing *BI*. His home in those days was in Hertfordshire, but both work and his interest in buses took him into many other areas, not least on outings organised by the Omnibus Society and other interest groups.

Birch Bros Ltd of Kentish Town, London, was always an individualistic concern and the batch of 10 Leyland Titan PD1 lowbridge models placed in service in 1946-7 lived up to the reputation, having bodywork built in the operator's own workshops, and of forward-entrance layout. Birch shared the distinction with Barton of favouring this entrance position for double-deckers in the early postwar period, a time when it had otherwise gone completely out of favour after a fair degree of popularity in the mid-1930s. The appearance was quite stylish, if a little harsh due to the lack of any bowing at the front of the upper deck – I believe the design was largely the personal work of John Birch, himself a sturdy individualist. By March 1952, when this photograph of No K186 (HLY 486) was taken at Hitchin, they had been displaced by a new fleet on the 'main-line' service from London and were used on local routes. In 1956-7, they became more orthodox, receiving Weymann Orion bodies. Alongside is HEM 488, a Commer Commando of Bygrave, based near Buntingford.

The replacement double-deckers purchased by Birch Bros in 1951 had full-fronted highbridge bodywork by Willowbrook, based on 17ft 6in-wheelbase single-deck chassis. Four were Leyland Tigers of special PS1/4 type and six were on Guy Arab III chassis with Gardner 6LW engines, including No K211 (LXV 211) seen here. It was photographed in April 1952 at the so-called King's Cross Coach Station – really no more than the cleared site of buildings bombed during the war, and one of a succession of far from satisfactory temporary premises for this terminal, used by various independent operators. Visible in the background are a pair of Leyland Royal Tigers with Harrington bodywork of the Grey-Green fleet of George Ewer, working on that concern's East Anglian services. Two Burlingham Seagull coaches, one on AEC Regal IV chassis, also just visible are thought to have been Northern Roadways' vehicles on that operator's Edinburgh or Glasgow service.

The location of this mouth-watering scene in these two photographs dated 10 October 1952 is not recorded, though somewhere in or near Hertfordshire or Buckinghamshire seems likely. The well-cared-for Gilford Hera coach, with readily recognisable Wycombe body, registered BLO 901, which indicates that it dated from about early 1935, bears the name Rickards, though whether it was still owned by that Paddington-based concern is not clear. The Dennis Mace full-fronted bus appears to have been of the type used as school buses by organisations such as the London County Council, though the registration, which appears to be DMF 964, suggests a Middlesex origin. The snout of a Dennis Ace, the normal-control equivalent model, can just be seen in one view, behind the Mace.

The star vehicle, however, must be the AEC double-decker in the background, which was the 1930 Renown 663-model six-wheeler originally owned by Northampton Corporation, VV 119, the body being by Grose of that town. When withdrawn in 1945, it was sold to Wesley of Stoke Goldington, possibly a clue to the location, though the lettering 'Refreshmobile' on the upper deck indicates a non-psv use. Almost as fascinating is the chassis, evidently a Daimler CF6 or possibly an ADC 423 of the late 1920s, visible to the left of the Mace in one of the views. The registration appears to be J 6354, indicating a spell in Jersey, though perhaps not when new. And then there are the goods vehicles, with a Canadian-style ex-military vehicle, probably Chevrolet or possibly Ford, on the right, and an American-looking truck alongside it.

Another scrapyard scene, this time recorded as being just north of Berkhamsted, Herts, in August 1952. On the left is seen HX 3507, an AJS, better-known as makers of motor-cycles and to some degree cars, but which was also quite well-known as a maker of light buses or coaches around 1930 – the registration is a Middlesex issue of circa 1930-1, though that county was apt to be rather erratic in its issuing of numbers. The AEC Regal in the centre is recorded by John Smith as GN 7277, which had begun life as one of a batch supplied to A. Timpson & Sons early in 1931. The vehicle on the right, of unknown make though possibly an AEC or Leyland, bears the registration GXD 791, issued in London in 1943 and clearly a case of re-registration, not uncommon at the time when vehicles that had been impressed for military or civil defence use, and of which the earlier history was lost, were sold off.

This Guy Vixen operated by the Sidmouth Motor Co was photographed in April 1953. The registration number reads as CDV 802 but should have been CDV 902, the chassis being a Guy Vixen new in 1947. John Smith's notes describe the open-sided body as 'home-made' and records that lettering reading 'Bristol Tramways & Carriage Co Ltd' could be detected under several layers of paint on the rear panels. In fact, the body was a rebuild of one built by Guy on an ONDL normal-control chassis of 1930, registered YC 9715 and placed in service by Burnells Motors of Weston-super-Mare. That firm was taken over by BTCC in 1933 and the ONDL used as an airport bus in the livery of Western Airways. The bus was sold to Sidmouth Motor Co in March 1947 but withdrawn in August that year, the body being transferred to the new chassis.

The Provincial fleet of the Gosport & Fareham Omnibus Co had quite a collection of interesting vehicles, but few as likely to mystify the onlooker as this. In fact UY 3186 was based on a 1928 Maudslay ML4 chassis and had a 25-seat coach body dating from the mid 1930s built by Grose, the same concern as had bodied the Northampton AEC Renown seen in an accompanying picture. It had been operated by a local independent, J. W. Main, since 1940 before being taken over by Provincial in 1950, by which date it had received a Bedford radiator of what appears to be a 1938 two-ton style, rather suggesting it may also have had a Bedford petrol engine. The juxtaposition of styles was far from happy.

This Lacre B floor sweeper was in use by City of Oxford Motor Services Ltd at its Cowley Road garage in July 1952 – John Smith saw it on a PSV Circle visit and had conscientiously recorded the chassis number as 271/12. It had a Dorman four-cylinder petrol engine. Note how the bodywork had been carefully lined out.

It was not uncommon for operators to fit secondhand bodywork to get new vehicles on to the road in the early postwar years, largely to overcome what could be serious delays. However this Guy Arab III with 6LW engine of 1947 of C. J. Whieldon's Green Bus Service of Rugeley, Staffordshire, was already on its second 'old' body when photographed in July 1952. It had entered service with a 1930 ex-West Bromwich Corporation Massey lowbridge body from a Dennis HS, but in 1951 received the 1937 ex-Birmingham City Transport Metro-Cammell body shown. The Birmingham architecture is self-evident but the cab front reveals adaptation to suit the difference in radiator height from the Daimler COG5 from which the body came.

The Tilling-Stevens petrol-electric models had been quite widely favoured for use by showmen, since the big engine-driven dynamo forming part of the electric transmission could be adapted to supply power for fairground use. Very few were left by 1952, but Douglas Corporation had been one of the last users, placing a final batch of the TS17A model in service in 1930. When withdrawn, this one found its way to London, where it was reregistered HYL 84 in 1947, and was seen in the ownership of W. Symonds at a fairground at Southall in April 1952. The Northern Counties bodywork appears still to have been in sound condition.

'Swords into ploughshares', almost literally. This ex-RAF Austin six-wheeler had begun life as a bomb-carrier, but had been converted to a coach operated by Ongar Motors, of Ongar, when seen in December 1951. The bodybuilder is not recorded but had produced a reasonably faithful pastiche of the Duple Vista body as fitted to the Bedford OB, which was widely recognised as the standard by which small coaches were to be judged.

CHECKPOINT

No 3: Cardiff trolleybuses

Born: St David's Day, 1 March 1942
Died: 10 January 1970
Main claims to fame: Second last new trolleybus system in Britain. Largest and last in Wales. Last British operator of six-wheel trolleybuses.

Why so late?: Perhaps because its tram system wasn't desperately old. Cardiff Corporation only acquired the Welsh capital's trams in 1902 and then had to convert from horse to electric propulsion. It was still buying new trams in 1927, seven years after starting to run petrol-engined buses. And there was an added local complication of a plethora of low bridges that demanded specially-designed lowheight trams which it presumably then wasn't in a tearing rush to replace. It showed some interest in trolleys as early as 1911, but took until 1938, when the tram system was beginning to wear out, to make firm plans.

And those were?: To replace trams with 10 trolleybuses on a cross-town route from the docks to Llandaff Fields. An order was placed in 1939 for 10 Leyland six-wheelers with 70-seat Northern Counties bodies – the preferred choice of bodywork as Wigan-based Northern Counties was owned by Cardiff businessmen. But World War 2 got in the way.

What changed?: Leyland was diverted into building tanks and other important military equipment, not Cardiff's trolleybuses. The order went to AEC which, although it, too, was being squeezed out of bus production for the duration of hostilities, managed to come up with the required number of 664T six-wheel chassis. AEC and Northern Counties designed the buses – which were delivered in time for the full service running from November 1942 – to cope with some peculiar local operating conditions. The chassis were insulated against flood water that was prevalent on the route, and the complete vehicles – buses and booms – complied with the 15ft overall height limit that had dictated the height of the trams.

Sounds like these were hardly wartime utilities: No, they went on the road with most of the opulence prewar passengers expected of their public transport vehicles, like upholstered seats and posh fittings. They had to be painted grey, though, because the pigments for Cardiff's crimson and cream livery were in short supply, and this drab disguise also was adopted for some of the city's trams and motorbuses.

A passenger leaves by the front door while others enter at the rear. The bus is Cardiff No 215 (DBO 475), a 1948 BUT 9641T with East Lancs 67-seat body.

Otherwise, they looked like trolleybuses everywhere else?: Not quite, for Cardiff pioneered a flat fare, no change, pay-as-you-enter fare collection system, first on trolleybuses, later also on trams. You put an old penny in one of two slots on the rear platform. The system absolved conductors of the need to roam around, as they supervised boarding and alighting and ensured that everyone paid the fare.

Sounds just the ticket: You may say that, but no tickets were issued. It seemed to be a success, and as Jim Joyce wrote in a *Buses* article shortly before the system shut down, it had the added advantage of bringing in extra revenue when the occasional passenger – hindered by blackout conditions – could be relied upon to pay 24 times the necessary fare by accidentally sticking a florin in the slot. He says passengers also clubbed together when someone didn't have the exact change. The next 55 new trolleybuses all boasted additional refinements to make the paye system work better.

And they were?: The conductor got a seat, there was a separate front exit with a sliding door and, on 50 of these vehicles delivered in 1948-50, a separate front staircase, too, which rose through the nearside half of the driver's cab.

Why not on the other five?: Like all of Cardiff's postwar trolleys, they were BUT 9641Ts, but these were single-deckers. They replaced seven ex-Pontypridd prewar English Electric saloons on the service along Bute Street from the city centre to the docks. A similar rear entrance bus came in 1955 and was the last new six-wheel single-deck trolley for a British fleet. It came at the same time as 13 rear-entrance double-deckers helped replace diesel buses on the Ely route, the only major trolleybus operation away from the tram system which had closed five years earlier.

And why rear entrances?: The flat fare went up by an old halfpenny in 1949 and was replaced by graduated fares in November 1950. With it went the paye system and, without it, there was no need for a second staircase or exit and most were removed after 1950.

Were these 69 buses also were bodied by a Lancashire company with Cardiff connections?: Yes, but it wasn't Northern Counties. East Lancs supplied them all or had them completed by Bruce Coachworks, a local subsidiary which previously was known as Air Dispatch.

What about the network?: It peaked in 1955 with 79 vehicles, but was under sentence of death from 1961, when plans were agreed to replace the trolleys with diesels by 1971. The first cuts were made in 1962 and the whole system shut down on 3 December 1969 when lowheight Willowbrook-bodied Daimler Fleetlines took over and 1955 double-decker No 286 worked the last 10A to Ely.

But didn't you say the system died in January 1970?: Well, yes, it did. The replacement buses arrived in time for the main service to finish a month early, but three trolleys came back into special service on the last day and for enthusiasts' tours the following day.

And why was No 244 Cardiff's most elusive trolley?: Because there wasn't one. Every other fleetnumber from 201 to 287 was issued to the fleet, but although seven numbers were left blank between 237, the last of the seven Pontypridd veterans, and 245, the first of the 1949 double-deckers, only six postwar single-decks were bought.

ALM

A FURTHER LOOK AT BIRMINGHAM'S CVD6s

The smooth-running Daimler CD6 engine could have been one of the all-time greats. DAVID HARVEY explains why it didn't come up to expectations

'What is that in front of me?

It is a Daimler CVD;

It runs so smooth, but burns the oil,

And has a tendency to boil!'

(With apologies to the late Cyril Fletcher)

With a three-bell load on board and the driver no doubt covering the brake pedal with his left foot, No 1979 (HOV 979) speeds down the steep Kingston Hill on Coventry Road. The bus is on its way into town on the 60 route from Cranes Park Estate in about 1962.
Photofives

THE STIMULATING article 'Maypole to Fighting Cocks', by Stephen O'Hara in *Classic Bus 24* about Birmingham City Transport's relationship with the Daimler CVD6 chassis, opened up a most interesting topic. It is a story of a manufacturer who tried with some success, to 'go it alone' and the nearby municipality which was 'in at the beginning'. Eventually BCT owned 438 CVD6s which made it the largest fleet of Daimler-engined Daimlers in the country.

The development by Transport Vehicles (Daimler) of its own diesel engine began in 1936 and although a unit had been bench tested, work was suspended after the outbreak of war. Daimler was still finishing off prewar chassis orders when on 14 November 1940 a severe bombing raid destroyed the centre of Coventry and 568 people were killed. The Daimler Radford works was largely destroyed and along with it the designs for the new Daimler engine. By mid-1942 Daimler had become involved in the development and manufacture of the 4x4 armoured scout car. It was also designated by the Ministry of War Transport to resume bus chassis production at the requisitioned Courtaulds factory in Wolverhampton. It was only in 1943 that the prewar engine design team, led by C. M. Simpson resumed work on the Daimler engine project.

Daimler, with its tradition of building high-quality saloon cars and limousines, had seen that the way forward was to design and build its own engine, which would augment the rugged, rather than sophisticated, Gardner 5LW and 6LW engines used in the prewar COG chassis. The new engine, the CD6, was intended to replicate the smooth running characteristics of a petrol unit while having all the economic advantages of a high compression heavy oil engine. The engine was extremely compact, being about the same length as a Gardner 5LW unit and the AEC A173 7.58-litre engine. But the quest for smoothness led to what proved to be the Achilles-heel of the design: the timing gears were placed at the rear of the block. Daimler claimed, as well as giving extra smoothness (which it undoubtedly did) it also led to more accurate fuel injection. The engine, when set-up correctly, fulfilled all these expectations, but this was not to prove the case in everyday service!

Just as Leyland's prewar engine was an 8.6-litre unit, so was Daimler's new power plant. The six-cylinder CD6 direct-injection engine had a $4\frac{1}{2}$in bore and a $5\frac{1}{2}$in stroke and could produce 100bhp at 1,000 rpm. By coincidence, Crossley Motors (of whom more later) was also at the prototype stage for its new HOE7 engine, which had identical proportions!

On test, the new engine, weighing just under a ton, was returning an average of 8mpg with five stops per mile. Encouraged by these excellent figures, six chassis within the 1943 MoWT contract for 480 CWA6 vehicles were modified to receive the new CD6 engine. These first chassis, numbered 12065-7 and 12074-6, were allocated to Birmingham City Transport, with chassis 12065 having only the fourth production CD6

engine. Delays at the bodybuilder, Park Royal, meant that the first of these CWD6 chassis for Birmingham was not received by BCT until 13 May 1945. By this time Northampton No 128 and Cleethorpes No 17, both bodied by Duple, had entered service on 4 May and 7 May respectively. The six Birmingham chassis were numbered 1420-5 (FOP 420-5), and entered service between 1 and 19 June 1945.

Top: ***Standing in Carrs Lane in 1949 is one of the Daimler CWA6Ds with MoWT-style Park Royal bodywork, No 1476 (FOP 476), that was placed in service in 1946. It is waiting to pick up supporters for a football special to Villa Park. Behind it is a Daimler COG5 and a postwar Brush-bodied Leyland PD2/1. No 1476, despite its youth, would only remain with BCT for another year due to the sub-standard condition of its body.***
Roy Marshall

Above: ***The effects of the recently ended war are all too obvious as BCT Metro-Cammell-bodied Daimler CVD6 No 1822 (HOV 822) leaves the pontoon ferry across the River Ems in Germany, while a new bridge is being constructed. The bus is on its way to Copenhagen for a British Festival with five other Daimler-engined Daimlers. No 1822 is being followed off the ferry by a Brush-bodied CVD6 (No 40, KMA 510) belonging to Stalybridge, Hyde, Mossley & Dukinfield Joint Board.***
D. R. Harvey collection

The performance of these CWD6s was carefully monitored by BCT and Daimler engineers. Initial findings were that the CD6 engine was everything that Daimler wanted. It was quiet to the point of sophistication, and apparently economical. Time would reveal the inherent weaknesses in the design. BCT engineers were initially impressed by the engine and in the last days of the war were allocated more CWD6 chassis. These were Nos 1475-9 (FOP 475-9), which were designated CWD6D, which showed that they had Daimler rather than Kirkstall Forge rear axles, and No 1480 (FOP 480), a standard CWD6, which was BCT's last wartime chassis. All six buses entered service on 1 February 1946 and again were bodied by Park Royal. No 1475 holds the dubious record of being the wartime bus in service with BCT for the shortest period of time – some 41$\frac{1}{2}$ months!

Postwar orders

Before World War 2, tentative proposals had been made to abandon the BCT tram system by about 1944. This plan was quickly shelved, so that at the end of hostilities Birmingham still had about 440 trams available for everyday service. The previously excellently maintained bus fleet, none of it older than 15 years, had been run into the ground during the war. The life expectancy of the standard prewar

Ah, Stratford, with the River Avon, crossed by the medieval Clopton Bridge, with its swans, willow trees, young couples punting and rowing on the river; the home of Shakespeare, the Shakespeare Memorial Theatre, fine acting, excellent food, wine and beer and of course the quarry belonging to Birds the scrapman, alongside the main road back to Birmingham! The fate of many Birmingham's buses was to be sold to W. T. Bird of Stratford-upon-Avon.

In this view no fewer than ten of BCT's Daimler CVD6s from the 1756 batch can be identified with Nos 1776, 1795 and 1818 (HOV 776 etc) standing awaiting their fate in the summer of 1964. Once the journey down into the quarry had been made it was virtually certain that an escape was not going to happen and of course none of the CVDs ever did!
L. Mason

Birmingham Daimler COG5 or Leyland Titan TD6c was going to be about 14 years, but many of the bodies, especially those built by the Birmingham Railway Carriage & Wagon Company, were in very poor condition and the necessity to replace many of these buses was becoming imperative.

The need to purchase new buses was a priority for the Corporation, yet the construction of new vehicles for the home market was restricted to a mere trickle compared to the requirements of the home operators.

The attractive, well-proportioned lines of the Metro-Cammell bodied Daimler CVD6s is clearly displayed by No 1989 (HOV 989) of 1949 and behind it No 1794 (HOV 794), which was a year older. Both buses are standing in Carrs Lane, with No 1989, next to the Bundy clock, working on the 53 route to Stechford, via the back streets of Digbeth. No 1794 is going to the same terminus, but by way of the main road route along Deritend and Coventry Road.
R. F. Mack

Their preference to continue the prewar practice of having Gardner-engined Daimlers was restricted by the availability of the Patricroft-built engine. Birmingham had built up a fleet of over 800 COG5s between 1934 and 1940 and although they had dual-sourced their fleet by purchasing Leyland Titan TD6cs in the 18 months before the outbreak of war, BCT was committed to the Daimler chassis, the Wilson preselector gearbox and the Gardner engine.

As early as 1942-3 BCT pre-booked provisional orders with Daimler for delivery after hostilities ended. The bodies for these Daimler orders were placed with Metro-Cammell and were all of the H30/24R layout. These materialised as 75 Daimler CVA6s, a relic of Daimler's wartime association with AEC engines. The new buses became Nos 1481-1555 (GOE 481-555) and entered service between 20 June 1947 and 1 November 1947 from Harborne garage. The MCCW bodies on these buses were very refined, picking up from where the prewar COG5s had left off, with lots of wooden fittings, moquette upholstery and leathercloth. Their bodies had a unique style of window pan which was not repeated on any subsequent vehicles built by Metro-Cammell. The CVA6s weighed 7ton 12cwt which gave them an engine capacity to body weight ratio of about 1:1, suggesting that they were a little underpowered. The CVA6s were withdrawn between 14 February 1961 and 31 July 1966. One of the class, No 1486, has survived to be preserved as the sole representative of BCT's postwar exposed radiator Daimlers.

Seventy-five Daimler CVG6s, numbered 1556-1630, (GOE 556-630), entered service between 22 October 1947 and 1 February 1948. The last four entered service 1 June 1948 as the original last four of the class were finished in error by MCCW for Newcastle Corporation and were replaced four months later. These were really Birmingham's first standard postwar double-decker and the true successor to BCT's many prewar COG5s, as by now the Gardner 6LW coupled

with a Wilson preselector gearbox and fluid flywheel was the Corporation's ideal combination. The prewar Daimler COG5 weighed 6ton 16cwt which with the Gardner 5LW engine gave it a engine capacity to body weight ratio of 1:1.03, which compared very favourably with the 1:1.08 of the 1556 class. In other words the performance of a five-cylindered COG5 was very similar to a six-cylindered CVG6. The CVG6s were withdrawn between 31 December 1961 and 31 October 1966, although 20 were lent to Wolverhampton from 23 January until 21 May 1961 at a cost of 6d per mile to work on four temporarily suspended trolleybus services. The long period over which withdrawal took place of these two early postwar classes was caused by the expiry of the Certificate of Fitness on some of the vehicles, combined with the need to dispose of surplus vehicles.

The next batch of Daimlers were the first batch of the smooth-running CVD6s. As with all Birmingham's CVD6s, they were bodied by Metro-Cammell and weighed 7ton 17cwt. Incidentally, this first class of CVD6 was going to have the body contract awarded to Burlingham. This was altered to Metro-Cammell, even though delivery would be delayed, after BCT's body manager went to Blackpool and was suitably unimpressed at what he saw! With the CD6 8.6-litre engine, in theory at least, they had the best engine capacity to body weight ratio of 1:1.10, promising a fairly sparkling performance that would be comparable to the Gardner 6LW unit. They were numbered 1756-1843 (HOV 756-843) and entered service between 1 March 1948 and 23 November 1948, except for the last member of the class. This was No 1843 which was exhibited at the 1948 Commercial Motor Show, rather strangely with the Brush body intended for Leyland Titan PD2/1 No 1715 (HOV 715). As a result No 1843 entered service on 1 January 1949. The 54-seat MCCW bodies on these CVD6s were slightly different when compared to the corresponding Daimler CVG6s. The

side cab window on the CVD6 chassis was short, while the rear dome side windows were longer than on the CVG6 chassis. This juggling act with the window lengths was done so that the longer Gardner 6LW engine could be accommodated within the standard 26ft long Construction & Use Regulations, while using standard-length saloon windows and components. All the CVA6s, CVG6s Nos 1556-1626 and Nos 1756-90 were fitted with handrails across the front upper saloon windows. After this the handrails reverted to a position below the front windows.

When new, No 1798 was fitted with very home-made-looking front upper saloon window ventilators which it retained throughout its life. No 1822 went to the British Festival in Copenhagen, Denmark from 30 August to 12 October 1948 along with one CWD6 and four other new CVD6s from other operators in the UK. No 1803 was re-entered service on 8 July 1949, when just over one year old, after being fitted with the prototype set of triple destination boxes.

Withdrawals

Withdrawals took place between January 1961 and September 1964 with mileages of between 375,000 and 440,000 over their 13 to 16 years of service life. Forty-eight of these CVD6s were sold to W. T. Bird of Stratford. It is thought that Birds had found a purchaser for 40 of them in Israel but the sale fell through, though whether this was because they had Daimler engines is only speculation. Still immaculately painted, though slightly down-at-heel, the buses lingered forlornly at the famous quarry for a long time.

The next batch of Daimlers were 87 CVG6s which were virtually the same as the 1556 batch. These were numbered 1844-1930 (HOV 844-930). They entered service between 1 December 1948 and 2 October 1949 and the first withdrawals took place at the end of October 1963. Many soldiered on into 1967 and 1968 with Nos 1923 and 1926 going in October of the latter year. These two were the last exposed-radiator Daimlers in revenue service in the city. The CVGs

were some of the hardest-working buses in postwar Birmingham and the term 'HOV-Gardner-will-travel' (terrible pun!) was coined to describe them. Many of them were associated with the Inner Circle service, being hammered around that route for most of their entire service lives. Some of the batch that were allocated to Liverpool Street amassed well over 600,000 miles. This might not seem much when compared to other municipalities at the time, but it must be remembered that normal service requirements in the city only used about 30% of the fleet, while in the morning and evening peak periods over 1,500 buses were on the road!

The next Daimlers were 200 CVD6s that had been ordered in 1947. Nos 1931-2030 (HOV 931-99, JOC 200, JOJ 1-30) had exposed radiators and were the same as the 1756 class, although they weighed 8ton 0cwt 2qts, which coincidentally was the weight of all later BCT CVD6s. This increase in weight reduced engine/body ratio to 1:1.07, so this was the same as the previous 1844 class. The first ones entered service on 2 October 1949, taking over from the Moseley Road trams which had been abandoned the previous day. The routes to the large Victorian villas of Moseley, the shopping centre at Kings Heath and the still almost open fields near the city boundary at the Maypole were most suited to the refined sound of the CD6 engine and the gulping noises of the fluid-flywheel. Deliveries continued until 1 February 1950 and most of the class had fairly uneventful lives on Moseley Road and Coventry Road, although later members of the class were variously garaged at Acocks Green, Perry Barr and Yardley Wood.

After two cycles of the seven-year Certificate of Fitness (like a strict MoT, but for buses), most of the class were again chosen for early withdrawal. The first ones were withdrawn at the end of June 1964 (with the exception of No 1945 which went at the end of March). By the end of the year, the whole class had been withdrawn! Nos 2021/5-30 were reinstated and No 2027 lasted until 30 September 1966. Their mileages were slightly less than the 1756 batch, but that is accounted for by them only managing 14 years in service. Four of the class, Nos 1956, 1961, 1965 and 1966, along with Nos 1841 and 1843 were sold to Oldham Corporation in August 1964 with the proviso that they were purchased only for engine spares. This was rather ironic as they became donor vehicles for vehicles whose bodies apparently were in considerably worse condition than the ex-BCT buses.

That is not quite the end of the story, as the Wolverhampton Corporation connection came to the fore again. A railway bridge used by trolleybuses in Willenhall was closed for reconstruction as part of the West Coast main line electrification. Twelve of the 1931 class were hired by British Railways from 24 October 1964 and 10 of them were bought by Wolverhampton Corporation on 25 March 1965. They survived until February 1967.

New-look fronts

The second hundred of the 1947 order for CVD6s were numerically the first BCT buses to have 'new-look' fronts. Deliveries of Nos 2031-2130 (JOJ 31-130) began on 20 September 1950 and continued until 2130 entered service on 1 August 1951. No 2033 was chosen to be the Daimler exhibit at the 1950 Commercial Motor Show, only this time a BCT vehicle was

exhibited with its correct body! These, along with the 2526-625 class of Guy Arab IVs, were the last MCCW bodies to be constructed in two halves. They were also allocated to garages where existing CVD6s were operating; Moseley Road, Yardley Wood and Perry Barr became synonymous with these aristocratic-sounding vehicles.

Yet once again the Daimler-engined Daimlers were chosen for withdrawal after the expiry of their second CoF. No 2058 appears to have the lowest mileage, only achieving 369,000 in just over 15 years! The first two to be taken out of service went in January 1965 and all had gone by 31 October 1966. Only one bus escaped immediate breaking up; No 2095 was sold to a Kingswinford contractor and was used until the summer of 1969.

In retrospect, BCT might have been better to have ordered fewer new buses for service immediately after the war, rebodied the wartime Daimlers (to which consideration was briefly given), so that after a normal lifespan, fewer new vehicles would be required in the early 1960s. BCT replaced its entire bus, tram and trolleybus fleet between 1947 and 1954. It then had a surplus of buses, which although not necessarily old could at least be identified as being less operationally successful than others. By the end of the 1950s due to increased car and television ownership it had become

The 2031 class of new look front CVD6s were ordered in 1947, but it took until September 1950 before the first one entered service. The body design had been tidied-up considerably, with the addition of the rounded concealed radiator cowling, full-length front wings, triple number destination blind and the sliding ventilators. The result looked more modern than the equivalent exposed radiator CVD6. The huge roof of New Street railway station gloomily arches its way across the skyline, while in the narrow streets below heavily-laden No 2067 (JOJ 67) rumbles over the cobbles. It is on the 48 route in Dudley Street and is passing the Midland Red's Parcel Express shop.
A. B. Cross

apparent that inroads into the fleet were necessary. The CVA6s and earlier CVD6s, along with the very non-standard RT-Type AEC Regent IIIs of 1947 and the 10 Crossley DD42/6s were obvious candidates for withdrawal. All three classes of CVD6 were to some extent replaced on a nine-for-10-basis by new Daimler Fleetlines.

The final batch of BCT Daimler CVD6s were ordered in the summer of 1949 when the final abandonment of the tram and trolleybus routes was announced. Along with the 40 Coventry Corporation KVC-registered Daimler CVD6s, these 150 BCT buses represented the swan-song for the Daimler CD6 engine. After a couple of CVD6s for Belfast Corporation, the model was only built in penny numbers and the CD6 engine was finally phased out in 1965.

The class was numbered 2626-2775 (JOJ 626-775) and had 27ft long MCCW bodies which were 1ft longer than any previous BCT buses. They were also the first bodies to be built in one unit as opposed to all earlier vehicles which had bodies built in two halves.

The first 35 entered service on 1 July 1951 as trolleybus replacement vehicles at Coventry Road garage. The last bus, No 2771, entered service on 1 May 1952 from Rosebery Street garage. The 2626 class were liberally scattered around the system being also allocated to Hockley, Liverpool Street, Perry Barr and Washwood Heath garages. With the exception of those at Rosebery Street, the buses were used in front-line service. Most of the class managed 480,000 miles in service, with one of the Liverpool Street buses reaching over 560,000. This was counter-balanced by one of the Rosebery Street vehicles, No 2766, which could only manage 364,000 miles!

One of the batch, No 2726, was experimentally fitted with a Daimler CD650 10.6-litre engine in 1956 and was demonstrated to Halifax Corporation.

The first withdrawals from the 2626 class took place in October 1968 when still in BCT ownership. When West Midlands PTE took over on 1 October 1969, no fewer than 104 were still on the road. Although the Daimler engine was by now regarded as obsolete, that so many of these vehicles had survived was a great advantage to WMPTE. New buses were difficult to obtain and many of the other buses inherited from the erstwhile municipal fleets of the Black Country had not received the 'tender loving care' afforded to the ex-Birmingham buses. The result was that five weeks into PTE ownership, 10 CVD6s from the 2626 class turned up in Wolverhampton, even being worked on inter-urban routes to Dudley, Bridgnorth and Wombourne for which they were not really suited. Some of these went on to Walsall to work on former trolleybus routes. The final withdrawals took place in November 1971 when one of the class, No 2745, achieved 20 years and one day in service. No 2707 (JOJ 707), has been preserved since 1971.

BCT and its CVD6s

Although the CD6 8.6-litre engine fitted to these vehicles had modified cylinder heads and were more fuel and oil efficient than those fitted to the earlier buses, their reputation for being less economical than other engines effectively ended their production. The problem with the Daimler engine was in the very design features which made it smooth-running. The timing chain at the rear of the engine made maintenance difficult unless the engine was first

This is the one that got away! No 2095 (JOJ 95) went to the scrapman in June 1966, but was picked up by Fletchers, a Kingswinford-based contractor. Fletchers, unaccountably, gave the bus the fleet number 4C! No 2095 was used for just over two years before mechanical problems ensured that it resumed its journey to the breakers. It is in Castle Street, Worcester on 26 October 1967.
D. R. Harvey

removed. Working on the principle of 'if it works, leave it', a timing chain failure had a disastrous result on the rest of the engine. Effectively the back end of the engine kept running when the front half stopped! If set up properly, or in 'tip-top' condition, it was a quiet, refined and smooth-running engine which when under a full load, tended to 'lack grunt'. If it was not carefully monitored then the engine tended to give off plumes of blue smoke and sound very out of balance.

Unlike Leyland O.600 and Crossley HOE7/5B engines which were positively Arctic, the Daimler CD6 unit did have a penchant to run hot, which further exacerbated its tendency to use engine oil, but unless there was a fault with the individual vehicle, then they were no more likely to boil than any other BCT bus.

When trams or trolleybuses were replaced the department attempted to keep to a 'one-garage-one type' policy. This policy did not really work where bus replacement was concerned, as for instance Perry Barr garage had Crossleys, Leylands, CVA6s, CVG6s and CVD6s! BCT never allocated vehicles to routes if the buses were not up to the task! For instance Moseley Road operated 1931 class and new-look front 2031 class CVD6s on the 49 bus route almost exclusively for over 15 years without too much difficulty. This service worked up the 1 in 13 hill in Leopold Street, which in tram days was considered to be so steep that it required a class of trams equipped with a special brake!

In other fleets that had received early postwar Daimler CVD6 buses, such as the Corporations of Bradford, Edinburgh, Leicester, Liverpool and Oldham, the relatively poor oil economy, maintenance performance and mechanical frailty led to the early demise of CVD6s.

Elsewhere, the contemporary Crossley also disappeared very quickly as generally the similarly-sized postwar HOE7 unit was heavy on oil, fast and loose with big-end bearings and made rich men out of cylinder head gasket manufacturers! Yet the 270 Birmingham Crossleys were built by Crossley Motors to a very stringent BCT specification. Many other operators got rid of their Crossleys quicker than their Daimler CVD6s, for example Bradford's Crossleys lasted only 10 years!

BCT persevered with their Crossley fleet. Although having an excellent synchromesh gearbox, again designed specifically for Birmingham, this went against Crossleys as far as the drivers were concerned when compared to anything with a preselect gearbox. It also had steering that usually demanded Charles Atlas-type upper arm development. On the other hand, the Crossley had a chassis that was more akin to a tank than anything else and had brakes that would usually pull up straight.

In Birmingham this relationship between the Daimler CVD6 and the Crossley DD42/7 is significant. The HOE7/5B downdraught engine used in the last of the exposed radiator Crossleys, Nos 2396-2425 (JOJ 396-425), and the 100 new-look front buses numbered 2426-2525 (JOJ 426-525), were fitted with this unit from new. The earlier class, Nos 2266-2395 (JOJ 266-395), had the less than perfect HOE7/4B crossflow engine, when new. Many of them were altered, with an ACV conversion kit, to downdraught specification and ran out a normal lifespan with the last ones being withdrawn in September 1967. Nos 2403-25 of the small class, were a prime example of withdrawal due to the expiry of their CoFs, being

No 2632 (JOJ 632), turns out of Darlington Street on the former Wolverhampton Corporation 4 route from Tettenhall. Other than the two 'native' wartime CWD6s and the ex-BCT vehicles, these were the only Daimler-engined Daimlers to operate in Wolverhampton. In this 1970 view, No 2632, despite its new ownership and operation in unfamiliar territory, still exudes its Birmingham origins despite being in its 19th year of service.
A. J. Douglas

taken out of service in 1965. The new-look vehicles entered service between June and November 1950, with the exception of No 2426, which took to the road on 24 February 1950 as the first new-look front bus in the country. Mass withdrawals of the class began in 1968 and two, Nos 2471 and 2505 just survived into WMPTE ownership. They averaged over half a million miles in service, noticeably more than the Daimler CVD6s of the 2626 class. This is in spite of dragging around a vehicle with an unladen weight of 8ton 6cwt 2qts which gave an engine/body ratio of 1:1.03, which was the same as a COG5! The preserved No 2489 is still earning its keep after achieving 555,000 miles with BCT and a further 27 years in preservation.

Had the PTE take-over not occurred, it seems that the new-look front Crossleys would also have lasted until about 1971, which was about the same time envisaged for the 2626 batch of CVD6s. The hitherto unmentioned short-length Guy Arab IVs with Gardner 6LW engines, from the 2526-2625 (JOJ 526-625) class were beginning to be withdrawn in 1969 before this process was hastily stopped. The PTE realised that many of the vehicles due to be taken over from elsewhere were in urgent need of replacement and these Guys as well as the 2626 batch CVDs would be needed as cover in parts of the Black Country. Within months of 'Wumpty' taking over ex-BCT Arab IVs and CVD6s were seen in Walsall and Wolverhampton with quite a number receiving the lighter Oxford Blue of their new owners.

The inference is that a well-maintained BCT Crossley engine was considered to be a better proposition than the Daimler CD6 unit, but it did rather depend upon the engine model, the age of the vehicle and which garages were about to receive new Daimler Fleetlines.

The CD6 in retrospect

In summary, the Daimler CD6 engine was an extremely refined unit. That it had virtually gone out of production in the space of seven years suggests that the engine 'was not right'. BCT drivers apparently enjoyed a quiet day's work in the cab of a CVD6, while passengers were carried efficiently and quietly; but it was not an engineer's engine! Half-hearted attempts in the late 1950s by Daimler to turbocharge the unit failed to tempt any prospective buyers. When the first Fleetline RE30 chassis was completed as 7000 HP in August 1960, it was re-designated as a CRD6, with a transverse Daimler engine. It was the only Fleetline that received a body to be fitted with a Daimler engine. Between its exhibition at the 1960 Commercial Motor Show and its first demonstration duty with Birmingham City Transport (who else!), on 9 December 1960 the CD6 engine had been replaced with a Gardner 6LX unit.

In Birmingham the Daimler-engined Daimler survived longer than virtually anywhere else. For example, the 40 very similar Coventry CVD6s of 1952, Nos 126-165, started to go in 1965, although four did last until 1972. Throughout their lives, until the final withdrawals in 1971, which was well into PTE ownership, all Birmingham's CVD chassis were kept in good condition and the Metro-Cammell bodies could have gone on for some time longer. But unfortunately the engines . . . were Daimlers! **CB**

HIGHLAND IN THE FAR NORTH

PETER R. MYERS recalls Highland's buses in Caithness 20 years ago

HIGHLAND Omnibuses' depot at Thurso in Caithness was the most northerly in the Scottish Bus Group and certainly one of the most interesting as I was to discover when I taught at the town's High School between 1979-81.

About 40 buses were allocated to Thurso and 20 to Wick of which about half were used on the contract services to the Dounreay Nuclear Power Development Establishment, which employed about 2,300 people, and was the greatest source of HOL's revenue in Caithness. There was a large contingent of lightweight Fords for the stage carriage and contract services and they were backed up by AEC Reliances,

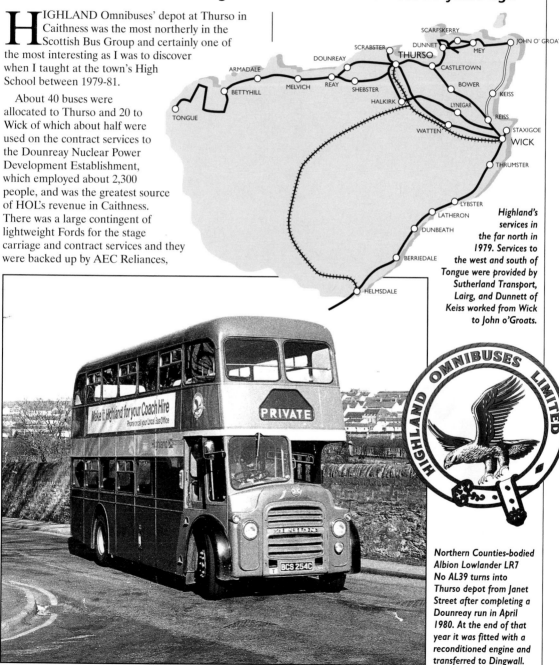

Highland's services in the far north in 1979. Services to the west and south of Tongue were provided by Sutherland Transport, Lairg, and Dunnett of Keiss worked from Wick to John o'Groats.

Northern Counties-bodied Albion Lowlander LR7 No AL39 turns into Thurso depot from Janet Street after completing a Dounreay run in April 1980. At the end of that year it was fitted with a reconditioned engine and transferred to Dingwall.

The Guy Arab III single-deckers with Strachans bodies were highly popular with the Highland drivers. A typical example was 1951 Arab No K90 which is seen at the Dounreay bus park in the company of ex-Western SMT Guy Arab LUF No GL11.
Roy Marshall

Highland's No B7 was one of the first two AEC Reliances in Caithness when it entered service in December 1957. It had a Park Royal C41F body and saw more than 15 years' service in the county. The two Caithness depots operated no fewer than 30 Reliances in 1972.
R. H. G. Simpson

Albion Lowlanders, Albion Vikings, an assortment of Bedfords, Leyland Fleetlines and Volvo Ailsas.

I was fortunate to make the friendship of Inspector Finlay Swanson, who kept me abreast of the latest developments at Thurso and who was also only too happy to reminisce about Highland buses of the past, going right back to 1938 when he joined the old Highland Transport Co as a conductor. My knowledge of Highland's buses, both past and present, was also greatly assisted by Jim Campbell, who was a police sergeant in Thurso and a lifelong Highland enthusiast.

Inspector Swanson was a native of Caithness and as a youngster had developed a keen interest in buses. His ambition was to become a bus driver and he applied to the Highland Transport Co at Thurso for a job in December 1937. He was accepted and started work as a conductor on 12 January 1938, doing his conducting training on Albion PKA No 47 (ST 6103).

Highland Transport had been formed in April 1930 and began its Caithness operations in July that year with services between Thurso and Wick via Halkirk and Watten and also via Castletown. Promoting its services with the slogan 'Civility and Reliability', Highland Transport was intent on providing an efficient and reliable service which it hoped would increase local trade. During weekdays a total of 15 return journeys were advertised, nine of them routed via Halkirk and Watten and the remaining six via Castletown. The journey time was a generous 80min compared with the 55min allowed in 1979.

Four normal control Albions with rear entrances were used to launch these services and a local newspaper reporter wrote enthusiastically about the Albions' passenger comforts, which included a saloon heater, well-padded seats and wind-down windows. He added that the low-pressure tyres contributed to a jolt-free ride.

One of Highland's more unusual buses was No CD13, a 24-seat Alexander-bodied Bedford VAM5 with accommodation at the rear for cargo and mail. It was exhibited at the Scottish Motor Show in 1965 and latterly served on the Tongue-Thurso route. CD13 leaves Melvich while en route from Tongue to Thurso on 1 November 1980. It remained on this service until October 1981 and was later sold for preservation.
All photos by Peter R. Myers except where otherwise credited

The most disliked of Highland's buses in Caithness were the 13 Albion Vikings which had originated with Central SMT, Scottish Omnibuses and Alexander (Midland). No AV15 came from SOL in 1972 and was withdrawn at Thurso in November 1980.

War service in the army interrupted Finlay's career although during a period of leave at home he earned £4 15s working as a conductor for a week with Highland Transport. This seemed like a fortune compared with his soldier's weekly pay of £2 2s.

Back on the buses

A few days after being demobbed, Finlay was back on the buses in 1946 by which time Thurso's allocation comprised of seven buses, including five prewar Albions – and an unfrozen Leyland Tiger TS11 and a Tilling-Stevens H5LA4 which both carried Willowbrook bodywork and had been acquired by HTC in 1942. The high demand for public transport in the immediate postwar period was also reflected in Caithness resulting in the appearance of the county's first double-deckers in 1946 and which were needed for the Wick-Thurso route. They were Northern Counties-bodied Guy Arab IIs, numbered 19 and 20, and the first of many Guys to serve in the far north for the next 25 years.

HTC's English general manager, Wilmot H. Fowke, was sufficiently impressed with the Guys to place further orders with the Wolverhampton company and a sizeable fleet of both single-and double-deck Arabs had entered service with Highland Transport by January 1952 when the company became the major constituent of Highland Omnibuses Ltd, the new, wholly state-owned company.

Finlay and his colleagues were more than happy to reminisce about the single-deck Guy Arab IIIs and none more so than No K92 (EST 395), which evoked the fondest memories among the Highland drivers. This 1951 Gardner 6LW-engined Arab III had a Strachans body and was often selected to perform long-distance private hire journeys. One driver said that once top gear had been engaged 'away she went, up hill and down dale'.

There were also vivid tales of battling through blizzards, especially during the great storm of

12 January 1955. Driver Donnie Forbes was undaunted by the severity of the weather and took four hours to drive Arab III No K86 from Wick to Traill Street, Thurso, a journey normally scheduled to take 70min. The conditions were so bad that driver Forbes could barely see the radiator cap let alone the road even with his face pressed against the windscreen. Similar bus No K70 was less lucky and became stuck two miles out on the Thurso-Castletown road and was one of six buses stranded in the blizzard.

'Bombers'

Underfloor-engined Guys also saw service with Highland in the far north, including the famous 'bombers' which were Arab UF/ Alexander coaches and had originated with Western SMT and Central SMT. The last Guys to serve Caithness were four ex-Western SMT Arab LUF/Alexander of Highland's GL class, which lasted until 1971. There were also some less endearing Guys, most notably the single-deck Arabs rebuilt by Scottish Omnibuses from ex-London Transport utilities and nicknamed the 'kangaroos' because of their notoriously heavy clutches,

The most famous of all the Highland Guys was No E72 (EST 392), the unique Arab III with Strachans full-fronted 57-seat body which was exhibited at the Commercial Motor Show at Earls Court in 1950. It was dubbed, perhaps appropriately, the 'flagship' of the fleet and did a spell in Caithness on the Dounreay services. However, the full front irritated drivers because the nearside front windows steamed up frequently with condensation and caused visibility problems, especially when making a left-hand turn.

No E72 was the last Highland Transport vehicle in the HOL fleet when it was sold to Orcadian operator James D. Peace, of Kirkwall, in December 1970, joining ex-Ribble all-Leyland PD2 ECK 934 to become the second double-decker in Orkney. Peace used them for school contracts and while the PD2 was later repatriated to the mainland, the Guy ended up at a farm on South Ronaldsay and lay derelict until it was eventually dismantled. I glimpsed its pitiful remains during a visit to Orkney in August 1981 and was sad that this was the fate of one of the most deserving candidates for preservation,

The affectionate recollections of Guy Arabs made me wonder if any still languished in the county, albeit in less than pristine condition. A colleague and I discovered the derelict remains of engine-less Strachans-bodied 1947 Arab III No K43 (BST 671) at Reay during one bitterly cold Saturday afternoon in January 1981. In its heyday No K43 had been a permanent fixture on the 34-mile Dounreay-Tongue service while similar bus No K70 was allocated to the Dounreay-Bettyhill run. No K43 was withdrawn in 1962 and went on to serve as a tourist information office at Berriedale and later at Reay.

First Reliance

The AEC Reliance also ranked high in the affections of the Highland drivers. Finlay had the privilege of driving the first Reliance, No B7 (LST 501), up to Caithness in December 1957 and therein lay a tale as I discovered from the January 1958 issue of The Scottish Omnibus magazine. Six AEC Reliances with 41-seat Park Royal bodies were due for delivery in the New Year of 1958 but an urgent demand for buses to take Dounreay workers home for Christmas resulted in top priority being given to the work. The first two Reliances were ready for delivery before Christmas

Willowbrook-bodied AEC Reliance BA20 originated with David MacBrayne and came to Highland in 1970. It was often used on the contract service between Thurso and the US Navy's communications base at Forss.

and were collected by drivers from Scottish Omnibuses on Friday, 20 December for the first stage of the 700-mile journey. On arrival at Edinburgh they were taken over by two Highland drivers for the trip to Inverness, which they reached on Saturday afternoon. They went into service immediately on arrival and left Inverness for Thurso and Dounreay where they embarked passengers and retraced their routes as far south as Newcastle in time for Christmas.

More Reliances came to the far north and began to supersede the faithful Guy Arabs. Among the most esteemed Reliances were those which carried 38-seat Alexander coach bodies and dated from 1961-2. No B30 (RST 450) was the first to come to Caithness and they were found to be ideal for weekend tours in the summer. The last of these splendid vehicles were withdrawn at the end of 1977, but I did learn that the body of No B34 suffered the ignominious fate of ending up as henhouse at a farm near Gills Bay, a few miles west of John o'Groats.

HOL had no fewer than 30 Reliances allocated to the Caithness depots at the start of 1971 but this had dwindled down to eight of the BA class in 1980. Seven of these were 1966 AEC Reliance 590s with 49-seat Alexander bodies which had come from SOL in 1969-70, while No BA2O (LUS 524E), a 1967 Willowbrook-bodied Reliance, had originated with David MacBrayne.

During my time in Caithness the Reliances rarely appeared on stage carriage services and were confined to contract and private hire work. It was in the latter category that I had a chance to ride on No BA11 (EWS 135D) in June 1980 when I accompanied a party of pupils on a visit to the Laidhay Croft museum at Dunbeath. The AEC was not in the first flush of youth but gave a smooth and comfortable ride, and it was little wonder that the BAs were voted the best and most reliable of Highland's buses in Caithness.

Lowlanders for the Highlands

Just as the single-deck Guy Arabs were being replaced by AEC Reliances, so their double-deck brethren were superseded by Albion Lowlanders in the mid-1960s. By January 1971 Thurso and Wick depots were able to muster 17 Lowlanders, which had come from Central SMT and Western SMT. As Caithness is sometimes called 'the Lowlands beyond the Highlands' the county proved to be appropriate operating territory for the Lowlanders.

The Lowlander contingent had dwindled to six in 1979 and all carried the more tasteful Northern Counties body instead of Alexander's hideous offering. They were numbered AL38-42 and had been acquired in January 1972 after having been loaned from Western SMT, and these LR7s were joined by LR1 model No AL49 in 1976. They were all new to Western SMT in 1965 and were the last of 193 Lowlanders built for the Scottish Bus Group. At Brora, 49 miles south of Wick on the A9, another Lowlander could be found eking out its remaining years on school contracts in the company of two ex-East Kent AEC Regent Vs and an ex-Maidstone Corporation Leyland Atlantean. This was Rapson's 162 NVO, which was ex-East Midland No 262 in 1978 and had appeared at the Earls Court Show in 1962.

The once-numerous Lowlander was an almost extinct species in Scotland by the start of the 1980s, and I was eager to ride on one before they disappeared for good. A civilian employee at HMS *Vulcan*, the Ministry of Defence (Navy) research and training

One of the many Willowbrook-bodied Ford R192 to enter Highland during the late 1960s and early 1970s was T51, seen outside Wick depot in August 1981.

establishment at Dounreay, tipped me off that he travelled to work on a Lowlander every morning and he reckoned that no questions would be asked if I made a round trip on the bus as no fares were collected since it was a contract run. I had a free weekday morning in May 1980 and joined him at the bus-stop in Castlegreen Road, Thurso. At 8.10am the reassuring shape of No AL41 (BCS 256C) hove into sight and we both boarded it for the 15min run to Dounreay. Among the passengers were Royal Navy engineering officers who would learn about nuclear propulsion systems for submarines at *Vulcan*. Leaving Thurso behind, the Lowlander tackled Scrabster brae which had always taxed the Guy Arab II double-deckers, especially with a full load on board. The US Navy's communications base at Forss was passed and before long the familiar dome of the Dounreay fast reactor came into view. At *Vulcan*, No AL41's passengers disembarked to be replaced by the homeward-bound night-shift workers.

No AL41 proved to be Highland's last Lowlander and took part in an enthusiasts' farewell tour in Inverness a year later. It was happily secured for preservation at the end of 1981 and left Inverness for its new home in Staplehurst, Kent, in January 1982.

Dounreay was the site of a Fleet Air Arm airfield during World War 2 and the UKAEA brought the aerodrome back into use for communications flights from Manchester and Liverpool. The aircraft were often to be found parked in the bus park simply because it was the only space available. This unusual arrangement prompted a picture story in the *Scottish Daily Express* in February 1971, showing a de Havilland Heron airliner of the Nuclear Power Group Ltd parked next to a couple of HOL AEC Reliances and an Albion Lowlander.

Most maligned

The most maligned buses of the Caithness allocation in 1979-81 were the Albion Vikings, which had originated with Central SMT, Scottish Omnibuses and Alexander (Midland). In 1979 it was hard to imagine that one of them, No AV5 (FGM 103D), had been used on the 120-mile Inverness-Aberdeen via Banff service eight years earlier when the No 5 Coast route was worked jointly by HOL and Alexander (Northern). While it was a comfortable bus to travel in, its lacklustre performance was shown up by the more sprightly AEC Reliances of both Highland and Northern.

HOL's 13 Vikings were shared between Thurso and Wick and were plagued by mechanical trouble. The garage staff were reluctant to spend too much time on then as they were earmarked for imminent withdrawal. They earned their keep by doing contract and private hire work, although one Saturday in September 1980 I found No AV3 (FGM 101D) doing a stint on the Wick town service. The afternoon peace was disturbed by the sound of its high-revving Leyland O.400 rear engine as the Viking trundled through the town bound for Pulteneytown on the south side of the harbour and home of the most northerly whisky distillery on the Scottish mainland. Back in 1965 this Viking's career had started in a blaze of glory when it was exhibited at that year's Scottish Motor Show as Central SMT's No AC1. Central's five Viking coaches did only one season with the company before they passed to Highland in 1967.

Another exhibit at the 1965 Scottish Show was Highland's famous Bedford VAM5 mailbus, No CD13 (CST 961D), which had a specially-designed 24-seat Alexander body incorporating a mail/cargo section. It was used on the Wick-Helmsdale route before settling down to the daily return service between Tongue and

Thurso via Shebster. The 2hr 30min journey along the north coast of Sutherland and Caithness was the most picturesque of HOL's routes in the far north, and No CD13's driver had the task of collecting the mail from 10 post offices along the route as well as many roadside collection boxes. The Bedford was out-stationed at Tongue and its driver took immense pride in his charge. It was probably the best turned-out bus in the Far North along with Alexander-bodied Ford R1114 No T157 (OST 257S), which was outstationed at Mey.

Similar Ford No T161 was rebuilt by HOL at its Inverness works as a replacement mailbus for No CD13 in 1981. It was a case of hail and farewell at the Lady Ross Hotel refreshment halt and crew changeover point at Ardgay in October that year when the northbound No T161 met the southbound No CD13, which was fortunately sold for preservation. No CD13 had been on hire to Highland's associate company, Peter Burr (Omnibuses) Ltd of Tongue, and a much older Bedford once owned by Burr could be seen at a farm at Larel on the Thurso-Watten road. It was NS 2283, a Bedford OB with Duple Vista body and still displaying Burr's green and cream livery.

Highland's assortment of secondhand buses attracted many enthusiasts to the north of Scotland but did little to enhance the company's image in the eyes of the ordinary fare-paying passenger. This situation began to be redressed in the late 1960s with an influx of lightweight Bedford and Ford single-deckers. The adoption of the poppy red and peacock blue livery in 1970 in the wake of the takeover of David

MacBrayne's bus services helped Highland to break away from its previous dowdy image.

Intake of Fords

Throughout the 1970s there was a large intake of Fords with Alexander, Duple and Willowbrook bodywork, and when I came to Caithness in 1979 the Fords were the maids-of-all-work. They were not only the mainstay of the stage carriage services, but also performed their share of the Dounreay and school contracts. The newest Fords were Nos T154-61, which were R1114 models with 53-seat Alexander bodies, and had come when both Thurso and Wick changed completely over to one-person operation at the beginning of 1978.

Buses to and from Dounreay were reassuringly full to the gunwhales in contrast to the depressingly low passenger loadings on the stage services in Caithness. I can recall travelling from Thurso to John o'Groats in a 53-seat Ford during the winter and finding myself the sole passenger after the others had got off at Castletown. The only consolation was that it was a fairly picturesque route as the bus negotiated the narrow twisting roads round by Scarfskerry and Mey before emerging back on to the A836. There were some fine views of Stroma island, which is part of Caithness, and of the Pentland Firth and its shipping traffic before reaching John o'Groats, which was cold, windswept and definitely out of season.

Drivers on the Dounreay contract services had the dispensation to carry the occasional fare-paying passenger, provided advanced notice was given at Thurso or Wick depots. I took advantage of this early

The Fords were the maids-of-all-work in Caithness during the early 1980s, and in this view outside Thurso depot are represented by Duple Dominant-bodied R1114, No T139, and an Alexander-bodied example, T91.

on a Sunday morning in December when I had to get from Wick to Thurso. I boarded Willowbrook-bodied Ford R1014 No T63 at 6.40am, which had a full load of parka-clad Dounreay workers. As the bus was routed via Shebster, I was dropped off 35min later at Glengolly Corner, several miles south of Thurso, from where I trudged into the town guided by the flashes of Dunnet Head lighthouse, the most northerly point on the British mainland.

The Sundays-only service from Thurso/Wick to Raigmore Hospital, Inverness was intended primarily for hospital visitors, but was especially appreciated by travellers returning north after being away for the weekend. Thurso's Nos T122 and T139, which were 1976 Ford R1114 with Duple Dominant C49F bodies, were regular performers on the Raigmore run. Both were turned out in HOL's grey and dark blue coach livery, complete with the golden eagle crest which added a touch of dignity and was infinitely preferable to some ghastly logo. The eagle crest had disappeared from service buses following the adoption of the Highland Scottish fleetname, but still survived on coaches and double-deckers.

I bade farewell to Thurso in March 1981 to take up another post. That year saw the departure of the last Albion Lowlanders, which were replaced by ex-Alexander (Fife) Volvo Ailsas, the first of which arrived in September 1980. No tears were shed over the demise of the Albion Vikings, although No AV3 languished in Thurso depot's back yard long after the others had left. The popular AEC Reliances also departed to be replaced by 10-year-old Leyland Leopards acquired from Western SMT. A more unusual acquisition by Thurso depot was Bristol Lodekka tow wagon No H10 (RAG 390), although Jim Campbell told me that Lodekka No L15 (GM 7022) had done a brief stint in Caithness in January 1970 and was the only Bristol double-decker to see passenger service in the county.

I made periodic return visits to Caithness and discovered that Highland's predilection for interesting secondhand buses continued during the 1980s. Among them were ex-London Transport DMS class Daimler Fleetlines Nos D50/1 (MLH 440/1L), which had originally entered LT service on 16 June 1973 and were allocated to Upton Park garage. They were sold to Ensign Bus at the beginning of 1983 and found their way to Highland later that year via Graham's of Paisley and Western SMT. Although they had been modified since their LT days, the pair retained LT's bullseye symbol on the staircase bulkhead as a reminder of their service in the metropolis.

I found another pair of similar vintage Leyland-engined Daimler Fleetlines at the Dounreay bus park in 1987, which had once been familiar to me with their original operator, Aberdeen Corporation Transport Department. No K942/4 (VRS 142/4L) were recent acquisitions from Strathtay Scottish and still retained that operator's orange and blue livery which contrasted with the red and grey colours of the Volvo Ailsas.

My study of Highland Omnibuses and its predecessors in Caithness proved to be a stimulating pastime as I gathered a wealth of knowledge about bus operations in the county, both past and present, and was fortunate in being able to share that interest with people who were equally enthusiastic about the subject. Inspector Swanson was a lifelong busman of the old school and it was an education to watch him preside over the operation of Thurso depot and ensure the heavy demands made upon him and his staff were met smoothly and efficiently. **CB**

CHECKPOINT

No 4: Premier Travel

Born: Cambridge, 1932

Parents: E. A. Lainson and nine fellow students who invested £50 in setting up their own bus company to provide private hires and, the following year, a regular summer service from Cambridge to Peterborough and Skegness. They called it Undergraduate Roadways and hired in vehicles from other local operators.

How did it go down?: No problems commercially, but the students themselves were in danger of being sent down. The university authorities – direct descendants of others who kept Cambridge's railway station out of the centre for fear of metropolitan temptations disturbing studies – took a harsh line against any students taking paid employment in term time, so ownership of the bus company had to be kept quiet. But the venture succeeded and, in 1934, Lainson – by then a fully-fledged graduate – was ready to become a full time bus and coach operator with his own vehicles.

So he set up Graduate Roadways?: No, the academic connection went and, as Paul Carter wrote in Capital Transport's comprehensive history of the company, the new venture was Premier Travel. The name came from the Premier Omnibus Company, an 18-vehicle independent compulsorily acquired by London Transport in December 1933. Indeed, this famous East Anglian independent could be said to have been set up with LT's money.

Why say that?: Premier Omnibus director Sir Christopher Magnay provided some of the capital to expand the new company which took over Undergraduate Roadways and two longer-established local firms, Royal Blue and Harston & District. They started trading in January 1936 with six vehicles, an assortment of local services, private hires and longer distance expresses. They soon had their first new coach, a Duple-bodied Bedford, but fleet strength remained in single figures right through World War 2.

But it got bigger?: Greatly. There were nearly 80 when the 'real' Premier died in 1990. A series of acquisitions led to rapid growth immediately after the war, although it failed to do more than snap at the heels of one neighbouring hound.

Why the canine reference?: Because it tried and failed to persuade Whippet Coaches at least twice to sell out. Instead, the two worked together fairly harmoniously and sometimes bought similar vehicles.

Did Premier's fleet change?: The small Bedfords were joined by larger vehicles and in 1948, Premier bought its first double-deckers, a Leyland TD1 from Oldham and a pair of TD2s from Red & White. They didn't last long, but double-deckers had a longer and frequently memorable association with the company.

How memorable?: None more than three County-class Daimler CVD6s with fully-fronted Wilks & Meade bodies equipped with such great luxury for their day as coach seats and heaters. The chassis of these coaches, named after the counties of Cambridge, Essex and West Suffolk, had been ordered by Dundee Corporation and the bodies were from a Leeds builder owned by Wallace Arnold, and which had supplied Premier with single-deck coaches since 1948. They were to have been followed by similar Leyland PD2s, but the Daimlers looked far

better than they behaved, so the Leyland order was changed to Royal Tiger coaches, before they, also, were cancelled after the manufacturer jacked its prices up by £250 a chassis.

Surely Premier did buy other double-deck coaches?: It did in 1962. By then, it had been through a succession of secondhand Daimler, Guy and Bristol 'deckers before snapping up 10 of Ribble's fully-fronted East Lancs-bodied PD2 semi-coaches. These were the original 1950 White Ladies which a *Buses Illustrated* caption writer had famously described as 'blushing' many years later when they first appeared, demoted to bus duties in mainly red Ribble service livery. Later, still, there were ex-Oxford Bridgemasters and London DMSs.

But no more new 'deckers?: Not only that, but there was a nine-year gap before new single-deckers came in 1959. The threat of nationalisation had induced panic and the end of the postwar travel boom caused Premier some severe financial worries which led it to be cautious. When it did resume new vehicle purchases, they were AECs, not Daimlers, Leylands or Bedfords and the company was refocusing its business.

Upon what?: Express services. Joint operations were developed especially with Midland Red and Yelloway, taking Premier's coaches much farther afield. And it bought a coach body few other independents ever considered.

If it wasn't Wilks & Meade again, what was it, when was it and why?: Wilks & Meade had pulled out of the market in 1955. When for the new design was 1964. Why may have been because Burlingham, the preferred choice before and for continuing secondhand purchases, had vanished into Duple. But even if we don't know why, we do know it was Y. The Alexander Y-type. Today, we think of that body mainly as a service bus, but in the mid-1960s its forward-sloping window pillars gave it a hint of American coach styling which obviously appealed to Premier. It bought 20 – including six very rare 12 metre Y-types – in 10 years, before switching to Plaxton.

What about its AECs?: It bought them until production ended in 1979, then turned to Leyland Leopards and Tigers, even MCW Metroliners, before eventually buying foreign in 1987.

And Premier itself?: It expanded to the point where the travel agency side of the business was far bigger than the coach and bus fleet and, in 1987, E. A. Lainson and two fellow directors sold out to fellow directors who wanted shot of the vehicles. The AJS Group took over, but sold most operations and 60 vehicles to arch-rival Cambus in 1990 and the remainder of the business – essentially airport services built up since 1964 – became Cambridge Coach Services, starting off with 19 vehicles. Premier became Cambus's coach subsidiary, but was drastically scaled down after Stagecoach took over in 1995.

ALM

One of the ex-Ribble White Lady coaches bought by Premier Travel from Ribble, No 142 (DCK 218), a 1951 Leyland Titan PD2/3 with East Lancs body, lays over while working the Saffron Walden town service. The nearside door makes for easy conversation between the conductor and his driver.
Michael Dryhurst

HUNDREDS FOR THE THOUSANDS

Summer days in Clacton recalled by R. J. WILLIAMSON

AUGUST 1959, a very hot summer and it's the first day of a holiday at a rented bungalow on the edge of the built-up area of Holland-On-Sea approximately three miles from Clacton. A short early evening walk down the main road finished at a small stone bridge over a river where half-a-dozen anglers were standing optimistically with their fishing lines in the slow flowing water. The gentle lapping of the rippling water and the chirping sounds of a few songbirds interspersed with the purring of the few, very few, cars were the only sounds to break the silence. That was until the five-cylinder Gardner engine of an Eastern National Bristol K growled round the sharp corner, accelerated down the hill, shot across the bridge and with the roadside grasses swaying from the air pressure, roared away between the hedges and fields in the direction of Great Holland.

It was only one of those fleeting 'moments in time' but the almost fully-laden vehicle showing 'WALTON, 107, (via) HOLLAND-ON-SEA, KIRBY CROSS' on its 48in-wide destination blinds, the immaculate green and white livery with black beading, the individual depot and fleetnumber plates, and the smartly attired crew all finally kindled the spark of a dedicated interest in the Eastern National company.

Although having an established interest in London Transport and Southdown the spark had been caused a few hours earlier by the sight of six Bristol Ks outside Clacton railway station waiting to transport holidaymakers to Butlins. The ECW bodies looked a bit square – not an unattractive feature – it was just that the more familiar rounded London RT bodies made a startling comparison. It is important to note they were not immediately recognised as Bristol Ks as 40 years ago there was little in the way of enthusiasts' societies or clubs apart from the PSV Circle and Omnibus Society both of which tended to cater for the older enthusiast. Much of the involvement in those

A general view of Clacton bus station. Although the picture dates from 1962 the vehicles illustrated were little different from those of 1959. The two nearest the camera are Bristol LWL No 340 (SHK 515) and SC4LK No 427 (604 JPU).
Photomatic

Dual purpose L5G No 300 (MPU 34) awaits departure on a journey to Tendring – probably on the 108. Many buses went around showing 'RELIEF' when they were not relief journeys at all. The black blank at the top end of the blinds was of insufficient depth so that most of the word 'RELIEF' was visible.

LS5G No 414 (856 ETW) takes on a heavy load for the 101B as K-type No 1337 (ONO 69) waits to pull out and head for Highfield Park.

days was very much in the nature of the 'pioneering spirit' although Ian Allan ABCs were very useful if you could get them. However, the class B1-hauled express from Liverpool Street had brought to Clacton hundreds of people – not all bound for Butlins – and this pattern would continue throughout the summer as it had for years before and, indeed, would continue at this level for several more years to come. Car ownership was clearly on the increase although most people still travelled to their holiday destination by train (or coach).

Scale of operation

A well-organised and efficiently run public transport system was therefore essential not only at Clacton but at every other popular holiday resort in the country. It must be appreciated that the scale of operation in 1959 and throughout most of the 1960s was immense particularly as Clacton was the only major coastal

resort where Eastern National had sole responsibility. Apart from Butlins there were, and still are, caravan sites of varying sizes at Highfields Park, Highlands, Valley Farm, Sacketts Grove and Meadowview. Added to these were numerous hotels, holiday chalet estates (at Jaywick for example) and other nearby holiday areas such as Point Clear Bay, Frinton and Walton-on-the-Naze. All of these added together meant a massive influx of people all away for a week or fortnight long before package tours to Spain became popular.

During the next few days an ABC (East Anglia Area) was acquired, a timetable was purchased at the Clacton bus station enquiry office and a study of the local routes commenced in earnest.

Apart from the 19, 53 and 77, all the Clacton services were numbered between 101 and 117 plus 121/123/125 whilst the 118-120/122 group operated in the Harwich area from Dovercourt depot which in

Bristol L6B No 328 (PTW 110) awaits passengers for an excursion – could be a mystery tour judging by the apparent uncertainty of the two ladies to the left!

Looking immaculate whilst laying-over in London is Clacton-based MW6G No 508 (3385 VW). It has just worked a journey on the busy service 'A' from Jaywick Sands and Clacton.

allocation terms often exchanged vehicles with Clacton depot. Most of these services, except at Dovercourt, had originated with the Enterprise and the later Silver Queen businesses which eventually became part of the Eastern National empire.

Some services were very sparse and only occasionally served the rural communities in the Clacton hinterland. The 108, Clacton-East Bergholt, only had two daily journeys each way and even one of those only went to Manningtree and back. At the opposite end of the scale the trunk route 107, Clacton-Frinton-Walton, ran a basic 15 minute service increasing to eight minutes in the peaks plus considerable duplication. This particularly occurred between 4pm and 5pm when passengers for the camps would finish their day on the beach or at the shops, make their way to the bus station and a mass exodus would begin to be 'back in time for tea'. The normal

service buses on 109, 110, 121 and 125 would often be duplicated though the largest duplication ever seen was one day in 1961 when a queue for the 107 stretched out of the bus station and down the road. The 55-seat Bristol KSW allocated to the departure pulled on to the stand and the inspector – realising that one bus was going to be somewhat insufficient – ran over to the drivers/conductors rest room and asked all of those present to 'stand-by'. The result was that seven extra buses were taken from the spares in the bus station parking area and, after swiftly loading, left for Walton more-or-less in convoy. What a sight that must have made trundling through the open fields outside the town. Considering the situation it is also remarkable that there were enough spare crews available to cater for this exercise but in those days considerable numbers of university students were taken on part time to cover both the busy summer

season and for full time crews on their annual holiday.

All the local routes passed through the bus station so that the town centre was served by every route. The open-top seafront service (112) pulled off the seafront, completed a double run loop via Pier Avenue and the bus station and continued to Jaywick Sands. Similarly, the 'inland' routes serving the indigenous population linking Holland-on-Sea with Jaywick Sands (115A and 116) or Magdalen Green (117) did basically the same thing via different roads. By getting up early it was possible to see a 107A which turned at Holland-on-Sea (Brighton Road) and this was sometimes accompanied for part of the way by a Works Service (often a Bristol SC) heading for the BX Plastics works at Brantham.

Vehicle variety

Bristol Ks were mentioned previously and indeed there were many amongst the 70 or so vehicles allocated to Clacton for the summer season. Many spare buses in the Eastern National fleet were sent to Clacton for this period which meant a great variety including examples acquired by absorption of other companies or simply secondhand vehicles purchased from other operators. Buses had come from City Coaches, Westcliff-on-Sea Motor Services, Hicks Brothers and Brighton Hove & District to name just a few. Some of the acquisitions included Leylands and AECs so that with the usual Bristols there was a great mixture and you never knew quite what would come along next. The most modern buses in 1959 were two Lodekkas, Nos 1535 and 1537 (later renumbered in 1964 to 2504/6), whilst the rest were KSWs, older LDs, LSs, MWs and SC4LKs. There was also a handful of the single-deck Beadle-Bedfords which were used (apparently) as traffic required. They were however used quite frequently on the 117 to

Holland-on-Sea and, if going to Clacton by this route, the family was informed that 'we are going on the little bus today'. They had the same 35-seat capacity as a Bristol L but possibly gave the appearance of being much smaller. At any rate, the Beadle rebuilds soon disappeared from the fleet over the next few years, the Bristol SCs were short-lived, the ancient open-toppers were entirely replaced by ex-City Leyland PD1s specifically rebuilt for the job, more LDs arrived and eventually the first FLF appeared. On introduction, the front-entrance FLFs caused amusing incidents as late-arriving passengers would run to the non-existent back platform to get on and, when alighting, passengers on the upper deck would walk to the back of the bus expecting to find the staircase! However, this is jumping ahead in time somewhat and what follows are just a few of the countless observations made in that first year or two of culture shock from the stark standardisation of the so-familiar London RT and trolleybus fleets at home.

There must have been some form of specific allocation of types to routes – in theory anyway – but often it was a case of using what was available. The 107 nearly always had 55-seat Ks or KSWs and great delight was expressed when an L5G was operating a mid-afternoon return journey from Walton-on-the-Naze to Clacton. Up the steps with the speed of light, sit on the nearside cushion of the full-width seat across the rear of the saloon and watch the kerbside flashing past through the open sliding door. There were several prewar Ks and a Leyland TD4 but the most ancient-looking buses were the open-top Bristol GO5Gs working the 112. These were by definition a regular allocation (appearing occasionally on 115A/116) and were only substituted by ordinary buses on some very

An anonymous Jaywick Sands journey is operated completely empty by Bristol K5G No 1256 (JN 9544) originally in the Westcliff-on-Sea fleet. Constructed in 1937 its ECW body was rebuilt by Beadle in 1947.

late evening runs or sometimes in the seemingly rare event of persistent rain. They gave a bumpy ride and much of this could be attributable to the concrete roads with tarmac-filled joints every few yards so popular in many seaside towns at this period. An equally but more prolonged uncomfortable ride was no doubt experienced by the passengers who arrived one afternoon at Clacton on a Bristol K on service 19 from Southend. The bus carried an 'SD' allocation plate so it must be assumed that it had been substituted for the usual LS or MW at the last minute to complete the 3¼-hour journey to Clacton. When the open-top ex-City Coaches PD1s arrived – with the luxury of upper-deck front windscreens – they were ridden on many times. The 15-minute service was very popular and on one occasion a seat behind the driver was the only one available. This was a different viewpoint and was made more interesting in that the speedometer needle bounced from zero to 30mph no matter what speed the bus was travelling. An example of mixed allocation was the 104 and 106 (Clacton-Harwich via Wix and Ramsey or Great Oakley respectively); one departure may be a Bristol K, then an L5G or maybe an SC.

Destination screens

The constant switching of vehicles from service to service could have caused problems with destination screens but to those interested in the subject it was a feast of variety. With the summer influx of vehicles any suitable blinds were taken out of store to provide at least something to indicate destinations. Not every bus had a full set front and rear – several buses had the

entire 'via' box painted out, some had both the rear boxes painted over and various other combinations of display eliminations existed. Many early 1950s blinds were still in use and carried destinations no longer used (such as BEDFORD and LUTON!), whilst a couple of even earlier blinds had 'CLACTON LNER STN' which dated them as pre-1948. Numerous Ks and Ls still had the 48in x 11in combined number/via blinds and most peculiarly had suffix letters for each short-working on trunk and some other routes with the numerous 19 displays going up to 19M and the 53 up to 53J. As a point of interest the only other similar examples of excessive use of suffix letters that come to mind were Crosville, Western National (at Weymouth) and Birmingham Corporation. As time went by, 41in-wide destination blinds began to appear – not only on the newer LDs and MWs for which they were intended but also on some of the vehicles with 48in-wide boxes which had the edges of the glass painted over black or green and some were even repanelled with a narrower rubber mounted glass aperture. After the service alterations and renumbering of 1964 most of the 48in via/number blinds were removed and replaced by a simple 10in wide number blind (giving a 'T' appearance as on LDs) with the aperture glass painted

Standing beside the impressive office/waiting room building at the bus station is LD5G No 1535 (1849 F) on the trunk service 107.
Fred Richards

over at the edges. One or two Ls however were seen still fitted with the old blinds but with all the service numbers painted out.

One area in which Eastern National did not have a monopoly was in the field of coaches. The company provided various express services to Clacton (eg 'A', 'N', 'P' etc) and used various coaches and dual-purpose vehicles. At the top end of Pier Avenue was a booking office/waiting room and parking space for two or three coaches which were used on day, half-day, afternoon and evening excursions. The excursion destinations were very varied and in common with many other similar operators any particular day's excursions were detailed on blackboards leant against the coaches and along the front of the booking office. 'Feeder' coaches were often used and picked-up at designated points such as Holland-on-Sea (York Road), Jaywick Sands etc and brought passengers to the rendezvous point in Clacton. Many different and assorted coaches were used including Duple-bodied Bedford OBs plus Bristol L6Bs, LS6Gs and later MWs all with various styles of ECW bodies. Without exception all the coaches at this period gave very comfortable rides having experienced day trips to Felixstowe and Ipswich plus an afternoon tour to Flatford Mill.

Coach competition

The competition in the town came from Cansdall

Coaches (the only remnant of the former Hicks Brothers of Braintree business not acquired by Eastern National with main Hicks business in 1955), Barnes coaches and the superbly turned out fleet of Suttons Coaches. The blue and yellow Bedfords of Cansdalls, the white and yellow Bedfords of Barnes and the red and cream Leyland PS1s and AECs of Suttons were a considerable contrast to the cream and green EN fleet and made a colourful addition to the town.

Final thoughts: The click-zip of a ticket being issued by the conductor through a Setright Speed machine (when 2d adult, 1d child fares were still possible). The sight of the conductor hopping up three or four stairs, removing the winding handle on its leather-bound chain from the metal pocket and then peering through the glass spy-hole to change the rear destination blind. Alternatively, at the end of a journey the sight of the conductor running round to the front of the bus, right foot put on the dumbiron footrest, left hand on the handgrab and then winding the front blind by the handle projecting downwards from the halfcab canopy.

1947 Leyland PD1 No 1117 (MN0 193) originated with the Hicks Brothers fleet and is seen at the Fernwood Avenue terminus at Holland-on-Sea. Over the years, and as the promenade road was extended, the termini at Holland-on-Sea had been Preston Road, Queensway, Cliff Road and Brighton Road and quite possibly one or two other short-lived ones.

R. A. Jenkinson

The numerous bumped heads of passengers sitting on the offside lower deck seats, getting up too quickly having forgotten the low roof formed by the sunken gangway upstairs and, indeed, the awkwardness of getting across four seats to a window position from the sunken gangway itself on the upper deck. None of this can now be experienced at Clacton, the Eastern National garage has gone, a 'full-size' bus is a comparative rarity and the bus station – location of so many hours of observation is now a car park. **CB**

Acknowledgement is made to the PSV Circle/Omnibus Society Eastern National fleet history for verification of some of the vehicle details and also to the photographers whose work has been used but no name appears on the reverse of the views themselves.

STAGE SERVICES OPERATED FROM CLACTON SUMMER 1959

19	Clacton-Danbury-Southend	111	Walton-Thorpe-Le-Soken-Harwich
19A	Clacton-Tiptree-Southend	112	Holland-on-Sea (Preston Rd)-Seafront-Jaywick Sands
53	Clacton-Tilbury Ferry		
77	Clacton-Great Bentley-Colchester	113	Highfield Park-Jaywick Sands
101A	Clacton-St Osyth-Point Clear	114	Clacton-Burrsville Park
101B	Clacton-St Osyth Beach	114A	Clacton-Burrsville Park-Clacton (Circular)
102	Clacton-Brightlingsea	115	Magdalen Green-Jaywick Sands
103	Clacton-Lt. Clacton-Thorpe-le-Soken-Walton	115A	Holland-On-Sea (Kings Avenue)-Jaywick Sands
104	Clacton-Wix-Ramsey-Harwich		
105	Colchester-Thorpe-Le-Soken-Walton	116	Holland-on-Sea (Cliff Road)-Jaywick Sands
106	Clacton-Great Oakley-Harwich	117	Magdalen Green-Holland-On-Sea (Fernwood Avenue)
107	Clacton-Kirby Cross-Walton	121	Meadowview Camp-Jaywick Sands
108	Clacton-Tendring-East Bergholt	123	Clacton-Manningtree-Ipswich
109	Clacton-Valley Farm	124	Clacton-Black Notley Hospital
110	Clacton-Sacketts Grove-Chester Camp	125	Clacton-Highlands Camp

OPEN PLATFORM

NIGEL ADAMS defends the record of the British Bus Preservation Group and looks to the future of bus preservation

HOW TRUE IT IS, the old saying about 'You can't please all of the people all of the time', the British Bus Preservation Group (BBPG) strives manfully against all odds to save examples of the nation's transport heritage – to what end? Why do we do it . . . ?

The BBPG exists primarily as a contact organisation; it has never had a policy of purchasing vehicles, although many will remember we have taken such action in times of dire need. There will always be critics, those who say 'why have they bought that old wreck?', or conversely 'how could they let that one go?' but our counter to these statements is always 'at least we acted, at least we did do something'.

By trying to take a balanced view we are guaranteed to make and lose friends quickly. There will always be those who feel we are not saving enough old (pre-1950s) vehicles or too few Leyland Olympians, so what do we do?

Regrets, we've had a few, but then again, too few to mention, as the song goes. But look at our successes: over 200 vehicles that would otherwise have called terminus for the last time have been rescued since our inception in 1990 and lived to see another day; finding storage, locating difficult-to-source spares, use of trade plates, preferential insurance schemes, two widely-acclaimed conferences – to name but a few of our achievements.

We accept we get it wrong from time to time. Our newsletter has been far from regular on occasions, although we have now resolved that problem. We bought AAX 284, the 1930s ex-Red & White Albion Valiant, found derelict in a showman's yard in Llantrisant, South Wales literally moments before bulldozers would have torn it to bits. Did we do wrong at the time? We think not. As one of very few Albion survivors, it is certainly no picnic to restore but at least it is mostly complete – however bad. Look at the scale of the work Mike Sutcliffe undertakes – everything is possible!

On reflection the vehicle has proved to be a millstone to us, we have neither the funds nor the time, so maybe it was a poor acquisition – although I can see the headlines in the press if we had stood by and watched it reduced to nothing: 'BBPG allows Historic Bus to be scrapped!'

Many of our members have raised funds to protect a particular vehicle from the scrapman's torch. Those vehicles that still wait for the day when restoration can begin at least have a chance. Once it's gone, it's gone; it is no use being sad or complaining then. Most of us are all realistic enough to appreciate that some vehicles will present more of a challenge than others to restore, and I for one do not underestimate the task. Funds and time are all in short supply.

But most importantly the BBPG needs you, the reader of books and magazines such as this, the person with an interest in our past.

This movement needs support, not critics. Many people have compared bus preservationists to the steam railway preservation movement, but we have differing goals, changing legislation and a very misinformed general public, many of whom have a jaundiced view of the bus industry.

We need to present ourselves, to show we are just as important as the National Railway Museums and the Duxfords of this world. People need to touch, to ride, to experience what was commonplace just a few short years ago. There are many individuals and groups who do just that, being seen out with their vehicles on the rally field and operating day.

But that is not enough. We need support from industry, sponsorship, political recognition that we are important. This does not come overnight or easily. Like respect, it must be earned.

With careful reasoning and balanced debate we try to encourage the sympathetic (yes, and sometimes the not-so-sympathetic!) operators/owners to ensure vehicles in their care are offered a future. We'll never save everything but we do our best to ensure a representative selection survives.

Remember just a few years ago when many rally fields were full of RTs. That number has fallen as vehicles have dropped away due to corrosion and disposals. The RM is currently enjoying a season of massive interest with examples commanding high values, but do we really want to see rows of them? We need a variety; feature the smaller operator, the independent, the less mainstream chassis/body type. Take care not to become the Stagecoach of the movement, all one type/livery hardly projects an image of the British bus industry that once existed.

No examples exist at all of some operators, Stockton Corporation comes to mind, and what became of the London Transport CR class, all exported to Cyprus with barely three left in existence. Only one vehicle exists from Luton Corporation in its original form. How many Southdown PD3s or Leyland PD2s do we really need to save? A representative is needed, not a whole fleet! As I said, a balance.

We must ensure all have their chance: a prototype Leyland National has been saved after many years in a breaker's yard. Will anyone save the first Optares, Leyland Lynxes or Wright-bodied Dennis Darts when their time comes?

From our conference was spawned the NFBCP (National Federation of Bus & Coach Preservationists) to be our voice to government and officialdom. Straight away I heard the critics, 'not another bl***y group, why do we need them?'. Well, all you dissenters, it's you this movement doesn't need.

The Transport Trust has considered the problem of what happens when a vehicle is left following a death; in special cases it can be 'custodian of last resort' neither ideal or something it particularly wishes to see happen; would our museums take it on? Again NARTM (National Association of Road Transport Museums) has aired this subject. There are locations to consider, a collection policy which may not allow a bequeathed vehicle to be accepted. Think about what happens when the current owner passes the vehicle on by whatever means. We all want the vehicles to survive after us for future generations to enjoy. We are only custodians in time. This is a subject that needs attention now, with a current estimate of over 4,000 preserved buses in the UK and growing.

There were critics of the sadly departed Norman Myers and his collection. Many, including myself, did not always agree with his ideals but no-one could fault his heart. He wanted to see those vehicles survive with such enthusiasm and energy it was infectious. Well, Norman is no longer with us but his buses all have been found new homes and may see a future. That is a positive action.

One day, in an ideal world or if we win the lottery, there may be a National Bus Museum which has universal motorway access in a central location in the country, has all the facilities needed for bus restoration and regularly churns out the next fully restored and shining example of our transport history for all to see. A shop that turns in a profit, free museum entry, running days every weekend, coach parties filling our parking area, capacity crowds . . . (A dream, maybe? Maybe not.)

But if you're not with us, possibly nothing will happen. So you can see from the above, we cannot be right all the time. Whatever people may think about us, useful or waste of time, we are there, we do listen. Only you can tell us what should happen in the future. Going back to our critics, we could pose these questions: Where were you? What have you done to alter the course of bus preservation? What have you saved?

At least we tried . . . **CB**

For more information on how you can help make a difference, contact the BBPG at 18 Greenriggs, Stopsley, Luton, Beds. LU2 9TQ (01582 413200) or send an e-mail message to bbpg@lodekka.demon.co.uk. Visit our website, via Dick Gilbert's classic bus page, simply type 'classic bus' or 'bbpg' at any search engine prompt.

'The RM is currently enjoying a season of massive interest with examples commanding high values, but do we really want to see rows of them?' asks Nigel Adams. These visitors at Showbus in 1994 apparently did.
Alan Millar